Dogs Say the Darndest Things

BOOKS BY MAIA KINCAID, PH.D.

Being Human & Loving Life: From the Wise Counsel
of Plants, Animals, Insects & Earth. January 2009.

Learning to Love: From the Wise Counsel
of Plants, Animals, Insects & the Earth. February 2009.

The Joy of Being Human: From the Wise Counsel
of Plants, Animals, Insects & the Earth. September 2009.

Dogs Say the Darndest Things: Are You Listening?
An Animal Communicator's Dialogs with Dogs. January 2010.

Cats Say the Darndest Things. 2010.

Wisdom of Love Publishing
P.O. Box 3156
Sedona, AZ 86340
www.wisdomoflovepublishing.com

Dogs Say the Darndest Things

Are You Listening?

**An Animal Communicator's
Dialogs with Dogs**

Maia Kincaid, Ph.D.

Dogs Say the Darndest Things: Are You Listening?
An Animal Communicator's Dialogs with Dogs

Design by Jane Perini, Thunder Mountain Design
Cover photos: Pam Taylor Photography

Library of Congress Control Number: 2009938463

ISBN 978-0-9822140-3-9 0-9822140-3-0

My gratitude goes out to all the wonderful dogs who have graced my life with their love, patience and wisdom. And to the caring people who have allowed me the gift of conversing with and getting to know their dogs through animal communication consultations and classes.

CONTENTS

The bottom line is that we animals love our humans. Our love is like that of a parent who loves a child no matter what mistakes he or she makes. We have a wonderful sense of humor as well. We love to laugh and we like to make light of what we can. In addition, we fear very little if anything, even what you humans term to be death. We have nothing to lose so we delve deeply into our lives and deeply into our experience. We live fully in the moment, embracing all that we have.

– Melissa, Black Labrador retriever

ACKNOWLEDGMENTS

When I talk with dogs, they naturally remind me of the value of oneness and community all at the same time. I feel grateful to them for their wonderful qualities of understanding, love, humor, compassion and patience — thank you dogs!

I would like to thank my students for allowing me the great pleasure of reminding them of their own natural abilities to listen to animals, plants, insects and the Earth. It is such a delight to feel their passion and excitement as they discover how easy it is to talk with animals and to access the love and wisdom of Nature that is so available to all humans.

When we listen to Nature we understand ~ the more people who listen, the more understanding there is in life.

Thanks again to my wonderful dogs.

Thanks to my clients for their openness and courage to hear and embrace what their pets have to say, and for the joy and wisdom I've experienced in getting to know them and their wise and loving animal companions.

I would like to thank Emma Clifford the Founder/Director of Animal Balance; in addition I would like to thank the generous sponsors, dedicated volunteers, the warm-hearted animals who have graced the Mash Units and the generous people of the Galapagos Islands and Dominican Republic who all contribute to the wonderful success of Animal Balance in supporting the preservation of the precious and rare species of animals and plants of these islands.

I feel grateful to my editor, Deborah Dobson. It is such a joy to work with her, and I so appreciate her creativity, passion and support in the mission of sharing these conversations with dogs.

I would like to express my gratitude to Jane Perini, my book designer. I so appreciate how she tunes into the spirit of a book and allows it to express itself through the design.

I want to thank Pam Taylor, my wonderful photographer. When I think of our photo adventures I smile because I enjoy them so much, especially the last one where we made the excuse that we must go camping!

To these three wonderful, creative and intuitively gifted women Deborah, Jane and Pam, thank you for the all the suggestions, fun, creativity and the joy of birthing our fourth book together! I feel honored to have become friends in the process.

My thanks go to Dr. David Milgram, Linda Ann Stewart and Dianne Hodges for their wonderful contributions to the well-being of body, mind and spirit and how they have touched me personally.

I feel grateful to my family and many wonderful friends for their unconditional love. Thanks to Joyce, Dale, Dev, LaVonne, Joy, Tom, Jordan, Jeanne, Lisa, Max, Chloe, Cameron, Ariana, Tracia, Karen, Betty, Mike, Paul, Gracie, Geneva, Josh, Terry, Flo, Bill and John whom I talk with on a regular basis for your enthusiasm and support.

I would like to thank the communities of Sedona, Flagstaff and the Verde Valley area in northern Arizona for their love and support. Thanks to the Sedona Observer.

Many thanks to the Sedona International Film Festival for all the inspiring films they have brought to the community and to visitors from around the world. Special thanks go to Patrick Schweiss, Debbie Williams, Lori Reinhart, John Snow and all the Board members and volunteers who make this possible.

I would like to express my thanks to the Zaki Gordon Institute for Independent Filmmaking, Yavapai Community College and all the school's inspiring young filmmakers.

Thanks to the staff and volunteers of The Humane Society of Sedona, The Verde Valley Humane Society, Lunch on a Leash, Red Rose Inspiration for Animals, The Sedona Dog Park and all the wonderful organizations that look out for the safety and well-being of our beloved animal companions.

Thanks to the local stores who have so eagerly and kindly embraced the wisdom and love of Nature shared in my books: *Being Human & Loving Life: From the Wise Counsel of Plants, Animals, Insects & Earth; Learning To Love: From the Wise Counsel of Plants, Animals, Insects & the Earth; The Joy of Being Human: From the Wise Counsel of Plants, Animals, Insects & the Earth* and now: *Dogs Say the Darndest Things: Are You Listening? An Animal Commincator's Dialogs with Dogs,* including: Sedona Hummingbird Gallery, Crystal Magic, The Golden Word, The Well Read Coyote, The Worm Bookstore, Crystal Castle, Sedona Pet Supply, Village Pet Supply, New Frontiers Marketplace (Flagstaff & Sedona), Compounding Pharmacy in the Village of Oak Creek, and the Sedona Public Library.

INTRODUCTION

You are about to have an amazing experience! Have you ever wondered what your dog would say to you about your life, or what any dog would say about living with and loving humans? After all, other than your human family, your dog is probably the closest living being to you. What you hold in your hands is a collection of conversations with our dear and loyal companion, the dog. You will discover answers to questions in life you may never have thought to ask, and what you may never have dreamed you would hear from a dog!

When I began my career as an Animal Communication Specialist about thirteen years ago, I imagined dogs would mostly want to talk about their food and preferences for their comfort and contentment. I soon found out that what they really wanted to talk about was the purpose and meaning in life for their humans and for our human species as a whole. Since I was a child I have talked with many animals, but it wasn't until I began speaking with people's pets as a profession that I was presented with one profound and enlightening conversation after another. The pet I talk with most often is probably the dog. They never cease to amaze me with their depth of insight into our human lives and the suggestions they come up with to the challenges we commonly face. I guess when we take into consideration that dogs have been our loyal and loving companions for thousands of years, it makes sense that they would understand us and that they would care deeply about us.

In my daily conversations with dogs, the information I receive goes far beyond just a simple desire for us to feel well and be happy. They lovingly dive into the core of our essence helping us to see, sense and know the real truth of who we are and our purpose in being.

You too, of course, can hear your dog and I heartily encourage you to listen! They want us to hear them and engage with them. As you join me in these dialogs with dogs you will receive insight from them into the enhancement of your own natural abilities to listen.

I feel so fortunate to talk with dogs on a regular basis. My heart warms at the thought of offering you this collection of some of my favorite conversations with dogs and of giving them a platform they so deserve on which to share their love and wisdom with us. It is with a deep sense of gratitude that I sense your presence here and invite you to join me on an enlightening and inspiring love-filled journey with dogs!

Maia Kincaid Ph.D
December 30th, 2009

CHAPTER ONE
A Dog's Love

I was about three years old when I had my first memorable encounter with a dog. My mother had her own dog grooming business while she was pregnant and during the early years of my life. What better way to be birthed into the world than into a home where dogs were coming and going to be loved and carefully tended? I like to think that this was my nursery. I enjoyed those early years and was a quiet baby who entertained herself nearby while my mother worked. One day when Mom was grooming a poodle, the dog's attention suddenly turned to me. He paused to look deeply into my eyes and into what seemed like my soul. I remember the power of his stare and how for a moment, it distracted me from my play. I surrendered to his lead and my eyes joined his eyes in a sweet and curious moment where it seemed as though the dog and I had become one.

As a teenager and young adult I remember having similar experiences with dogs, but not feeling so comfortable about them.

1

I had become accustomed to relating with my fellow humans in a shallow sort of way. So when a dog locked onto me with a loving stare, he or she was asking me to go deep and I felt naked and exposed. I resisted and would look away, but then I felt compelled to look back and when I did, I would feel comfort and safety in the dog's love. I would remember that this was my loving companion and I would surrender and enjoy a few moments of oneness and true love with a fellow being of life.

I'm sure many of you have experienced moments like the ones I just described of simple yet profound connecting. Dogs touch us with their unique personalities, their antics, mischievousness, their stability, their wisdom, their peacefulness, their patience, and perhaps more than anything, they touch us with their love.

When most of us pause to ponder the animal we call the dog we agree there's something amazing about them. From my childhood and throughout my life I've wondered who they really are and what makes them so interesting. They've captured my curiosity with all their enthusiasm for life and the way they joyously greet a new human or a new day. Even when we don't know them personally, they often show us their unconditional love and affection. I like to think of dogs as fine ambassadors for life, as teachers and loving companions who guide, nurture and love us along the way.

Dogs have become integral to our human lives. We have shared a long history together of at least 14,000 years and during that time, they have played many roles and served us devotedly, but they have always been our loyal, loving companions. They are as popular today as ever or perhaps even more popular. Dogs are a part of our lives, even if we don't have a dog. We see them wherever we go accompanying their humans in their daily travels. People sometimes even talk of their dogs as being their soul mates, or the love of their lives.

Dogs contribute to our well-being with their loving presence in many ways; they are often responsible for our daily exercise when we take them for a walk. Sometimes they are the basis of our social networking with the formation of many dog-loving social groups and dog parks where people can allow their dogs to exercise, play and interact with other dogs while they connect with fellow dog-loving humans.

Nowadays dogs often represent our main connection with the natural world. Many people live in cities and work all day inside buildings, and even those who live in smaller towns tend to work indoors. Often, the only reason they are outdoors in Nature at all is to take their dog for a walk. Our dogs represent Nature itself — they're like a living symbol that reminds us every day of the roots of our existence and who we really are. There is something profound and completely genuine in their way of being. Their loving presence comforts us when we're feeling low, they stabilize us when we're feeling scattered and they remind us of the simple truth of life.

Dogs remind us that we too, are animals and that when we are involved in simple, natural activities we often feel the most peaceful and content. They bring us back to our senses and remind us that we are loved, and that life doesn't have to be so serious and such a challenge. They help us remember what's really important. They are some of my greatest teachers.

I am very fortunate to work in a profession that allows me

to interact with dogs from around the world each day. I am an Animal Communication Specialist so I talk with animals of many species, but the dog is probably the animal I talk with most often. People ask me to talk with their canine friends about new and unusual behaviors, health issues, the animal's diet and preferences for activities, travel, vacations, and transitions, including the transition of death. My passion is to help people listen to their own dogs and to all the life around them.

My adventure of communicating with dogs began out of my own need to find contentment in being human. Even though my young life was filled with my mother's dog grooming clients, as a child and even as a young adult I felt uncomfortable and confused in my human interactions. I was extremely shy and sensitive. I often felt like I was another species in a human body or at least from another planet. When I thought of becoming an adult, I did not feel enthusiastic. To me, adults seemed so stressed and overwhelmed in their day-to-day lives. I remember looking at the way people lived and thinking, "This can't be it, there has to be more to life than this!" I noticed there was little natural creativity, joy and passion for living in most of the people I observed. And there were all these things that seemed to be so important, like what someone was wearing, how they looked, what they said and where they lived. I found this all to be very confusing. It seemed as though there was a set of artificial rules and goals that people stressed over and struggled to achieve, but that in the end had little appeal and gave virtually no satisfaction.

As a child, none of this made any sense to me. What made sense to me was that I could simply be myself when I was with dogs or in Nature. Nothing that seemed so important to humans mattered at all to dogs. They didn't care what clothes I wore, what I said, how I moved, how my body looked or where I lived. Instead, they loved me no matter what and they never let me forget that I was loved. Dogs did not judge me and they freely gave their love with no expectation of anything in return.

Knowing that I was loved just as I was didn't help me initially fit into the human world because this concept did not seem to be true in the world of humans. Simply being was not enough — I had to do something, be something and have something. I naturally wanted to fit in and be like others but it never seemed to work. When I tried to be someone or something other than myself I had an uncomfortable feeling of not being true to myself, to my own unique spirit. After struggling with this for years, I finally realized that what I had learned from dogs about just being myself really is the true way. I stopped trying to fit in. As long as I lived in this reality of the truth that I was fine just the way I was, I could live in the human world with relative ease and comfort and even joy and grace.

Because of the confusion I felt about my purpose in being and what life as a human was really all about, I naturally looked to the wise and knowing presence of dogs and other beings of Nature for answers to my questions about life. I talked with animals all the time in my daily life and I noticed that I felt most content when I was with animals or out in Nature.

It was an enlightening experience with a friend named Dan that inspired me to begin having formal dialogs with animals. Dan and his wife Carolyn were my good friends and skiing buddies. One day on the way down from Mt. Bachelor after a beautiful day of skiing in central Oregon, Dan began talking about intuition and mentioned that he thought I had some intuitive gifts. He casually offered to work with me sometime if I was interested. I was!

A few days later I was sitting in Dan and Carolyn's living room and Dan asked me to use my intuition to look into a current challenge he was experiencing with his throat. I began asking my intuition about his throat and instantly received responses that I shared with him. He immediately commented that I already knew how to do this, that I just hadn't realized it. I was amazed at how clear the information was and how comfortable I felt in receiving it. This new awareness was a turning point in my life. I had always been a very sensitive person and felt everyone's unexpressed emotions and pain. I often felt confused about what I was sensing and why I was sensing it. I had isolated myself even as a child in order to find relief from the over-stimulation coming from my human environment.

When I realized that I could ask my intuition questions and receive clear responses, I was ecstatic. I immediately put this to work in my day-to-day life to help me discern if what I was sensing was my own stuff or the emotions, physical pain or issues I might have picked up from another human. Almost right away, I began to feel a true sense of myself, and within weeks I was feeling more inner peace and clarity. In addition to asking myself how I was feeling, I also began talking with my own cells and organs and realized the joy and the value of knowing myself in a more intimate way and understanding what had me feeling most alive and passionate about my adventure of life.

I soon had the thought that I could ask my own self about the nutrients I needed and about decisions for my life. It then occurred to me that I could ask animals all the things I so wanted to know. I had been communing with Nature all along, but now I had the idea of asking direct questions and knowing that I could expect a response. I could ask the majestic trees and the tiny delicate flowering plants and the celery I was about to eat and even the rose bush! I was overjoyed about discovering this doorway that opened to a new world. It seemed so easy — always right there available to me — and to everyone!

I began by asking some direct questions and listening quietly to my dog Winston, who had passed away years earlier. As he responded to my questions about his life with my family I felt a profound sense of love, gratitude and joy emanating from him as we talked. I had never felt such powerful feelings of joy before. I talked with my horse Delight, who lived with me at the time and felt a whole different feeling with him as he shared his wisdom on what it was like to be a horse, what he would like humans to understand about living with horses and about life.

All I had to do was think of the animal, say hello (just as I would to a human) and I instantly began to feel the animal's personality, their playfulness, shyness or their wise, loving nature. I would feel their level of contentment as a wave of love washing over me, or I would feel their sadness or fear. It was as if we had become one, simply in the desire to communicate.

After my greeting, I would then ask the animal questions about his or her life. Was he happy? Did she like her food? Was there anything they wanted to express to their humans?

Soon after I began having these dialogs with animals, people heard about them and started to call on me to talk with their pets. They gave me the name of their animal and shared their concerns about a new behavior, an illness and their questions about how to make their beloved pet more comfortable and content. Before beginning my dialogue, I would pause to focus on my breath and clear my mind of whatever I had been thinking about previously. Then I would simply greet the animal by saying, "Hello..." and their name in my head. Instantly, I sensed the presence of another being of life, much like when we sense the arrival of another person, although we may not see them.

Along with the animal's presence also came their personality, their likes and dislikes, their loves — including the love of their humans. I felt a sense of their lifestyle, too — the peacefulness or the stress and how they felt in their world. The information from them came in feelings like powerful emotions that would go through me. I also sometimes saw images of how they might define their form or shape, an unusual way they moved or something they liked to do with their human. The information came intuitively — I knew without knowing why or how, but I knew without question nevertheless.

For instance, I might ask someone's pet a question, receive an unexpected response followed by an unquestionable knowing that this was the truth. Then the animal would explain why it was the truth and it made perfect sense.

I would sometimes hear words in my head and there were often phrases, whole sentences and paragraphs. I recorded pages of expressions of their truth, which came to me with great passion and feeling that seemed to stay with me long after our conversation had concluded.

I wondered how I could receive messages and responses in my own language and how the animals corrected my use of words by guiding me to a word that better explained what they were trying to say. I still don't entirely understand how this works, but once I asked a raven, "How do you communicate to me in my own language?" She explained that she expressed herself clearly in her own language and that my brain translated it into my language. A part of the communication and translation process was listening for any correction in the information I received, which might involve asking the animal further questions to be sure the meaning was right. Over the years, I have found that I prefer to carry on a conversation while either typing in my questions and the responses or by taking notes on paper in the same way. I don't always record the conversations — sometimes I just listen and talk but sometimes, because animals say the most surprising and amazing things, I like to be able to take down the information so that I may read it again later or share it. As easily as I began to do this work, it soon became a way of life and a profession for me where people from around the world contacted me to talk with their pets. Joining with the animals in this profound way is such a joy. I feel their passion for life and their love for their humans. I feel grateful and inspired and am continuously reminded of my own blessings.

So, without seeing them in the physical sense, I receive information from animals. We humans call this telepathic communication. I have often heard animals say that when we commune in this way, we have joined in what they call collective mind, where all that is known by one can be shared with the other and vice versa. It is not that everything is discussed, but that in coming together, all is available to one another. The animals have guided me in focusing on the moment and the conversation as if there is nothing else going on in the world. They remind me that all there is in any given moment is myself and another fellow being of life, and of the importance of placing all my attention on giving and receiving energy – sharing – with another. They encourage us to consider doing this whether we are talking with our best friend, a checker at the grocery store, our grandfather, our child or with our dog. If we're doing something else or thinking about something else while talking with another, we are not really there, we are not really communicating and we miss so much. In this way of communicating with dogs and other animals I have learned to appreciate moments of oneness communicating with people too.

During my conversations with dogs over the years, I have come to understand that we are deeply connected to our animals and that they often mirror very clearly what is going on inside us and what we might rather not acknowledge or face. For instance, I recently talked with a dog named Denny who I was told had a urinary challenge and some behavioral problems as well. However, after a short conversation with Denny, I had an entire list of information for his human on how she could experience more joy and a sense of aliveness and how this in turn would not only positively impact her own physical health, including certain organs and organ systems, but also the organs of her dog! Specifically, Denny told me that his heart literally felt stagnant as if there was little muscle tone or activity. Looking at it from an emotional standpoint, it barely kept going because there was very little joy or love being circulated. Although Denny's woman loved him and treated him well, their life was very controlled and there was a lot of fear. Even Denny's kidneys spoke up and asked to be thought of with love. They asked his woman to imagine holding them one at a time in the palm of her hand and feeling love and compassion for them. Denny explained that the kidneys are the base or foundation of the physical body of a living being. His digestive organs also reported that they were not digesting life well. Apparently, his woman negatively judged and was afraid of many of the foods she and her dog continued to eat. Her fears regularly caused Denny's digestive system to halt its work and then start again. Overall, it made for poor digestion and assimilation of nutrients for both the dog and the woman.

And then there was Benjy, Brenda's beloved dog who had re-injured his leg for the second time in a year after nine months of grueling recovery from the first incident. The day I talked with Benjy, Brenda commented that she herself was feeling ill. But when I tried to ask Benjy questions about what might be helpful for him in healing his leg, he refused to talk about that until after he'd given the information he wanted to share in regard to Brenda. His first comment was that his own healing was dependent upon hers, and that she had been feeling depressed and tired for a few years now. He continued by saying that his human was not listening to herself, that she was not listening to the wisdom of her highest awareness and to the simple suggestions she heard on a daily basis to nurture her heart and soul. Benjy said that like many of us, Brenda kept herself busy with mundane tasks and failed to follow through with her passions which in turn caused her to become stagnant and literally immobilized in her life and so had he! Because of his injury, he had to be kept in a small confined space but it seemed he never fully healed. Benjy reminded me once again that his full recovery depended on his woman's willingness to listen to herself and to take the action she was guided to take in her life by her own awareness.

I have had probably hundreds of conversations with dogs over the years and many fond memories and snippets of information have stayed with me. For instance, a dog named Niner requested that his humans think of him as a roommate instead of "The Dog".

And then there was Jack, a faithful companion to his man, who became a three-legged dog when it was necessary to remove one of his hind legs. Before the surgery, I asked Jack how he felt about losing his leg, the new life he would be faced with and whether he wanted to go through the operation. He indicated that he understood and agreed to have the surgery. When I talked with Jack to check in with him afterward, his immediate concern was for his human and how he was feeling about this change. Jack wanted to be sure that he was handling this transition well. In our conversation, Jack let me know that he was fine. For him, the truth was that he now had three legs and it was as if he always had three legs. He did not think, "I've lost a leg" he thought, "I have three legs" like that was something to be grateful for. Jack was actually having fun figuring out how to do everything with three legs. For him, it was a new adventure that he dove into fully and that he enjoyed. Jack adapted amazingly well and became an inspiration to all those who knew him.

Today I continue to enjoy talking with and listening to people's pets, and I have discovered my passion to help others awaken their own natural listening abilities through simple exercises and fun practices. I firmly believe that all humans have these innate capabilities and having made numerous and profound changes in my own life that have brought me greater peace and joy based on the conversations I've been privileged to enjoy, I naturally want to share this with others.

When I work with my clients, it is a very natural experience. Each person has their unique interests and passions. For instance, one of my clients has a dog and a cat and she is a skilled practitioner of Chinese Medicine, using Asian herbs. We easily and naturally talk with her two pets as well as the herbs she grows in her garden and the ones she utilizes in her practice. In addition, she receives guidance in our sessions in talking with her own body, mind and spirit with regard to whatever challenges and joys come her way. Whatever is going on in her life, whether it be with her personally, one of her pets, questions about the use of herbs or making herbal remedies or even looking in on whether to use a particular plant for one of her clients is great material with which to intuitively approach the situation. It helps bring resolution and peace while allowing her to gain confidence and new skills that help in the next challenge. My clients comment on having more peace and comfort in their journey of life, and they often share their passion for all the interesting things they begin to understand and experience. My goal is to empower people with the skills to comfortably inspire their own journey. The questions in our lives are endless and the answers are right at our fingertips when we open ourselves to our highest wisdom by pausing to ask questions and allow the responses to come forth.

In addition to talking with animals, I also enjoy conversing with plants, insects and the Earth itself. Their love and wisdom has been a wonderful blessing that has helped me find my purpose, passion for the adventure of life and joy in simply being. The conversations that have touched me most deeply and that I attribute to changing my life in a beautiful way have been shared here in this book and in three books published in 2009 called: *Being Human & Loving Life: From the Wise Counsel of Plants, Animals, Insects & Earth; Learning to Love: From the Wise Counsel of Plants, Animals, Insects & the Earth;* and *The Joy of Being Human: From the Wise Counsel of Plants, Animals, Insects & the Earth.*

In the early days of my career in animal communication, I believed I would receive information from the animals that was based on their particular needs for contentment and well-being. I was then quite surprised when I began to receive information from animals to specifically benefit both their particular humans and humanity as a whole. I was touched by the profound truths conveyed in their messages that they shared with such love, compassion, humor and understanding for our species. One consistent message I've received from them is their desire that we humans find joy and real contentment in simply being human — the kind of almost decadent contentment we notice in a dog.

The first message that really captured my attention and the one that brought me quickly to the understanding that it was important for me to save them and to one day share them with my fellow humans was from a dog named Kanoe. In this conversation though, I knew something was different when Kanoe paused to make an important point that this was not a message just for her human, but a message for all humans. She went on to say that she was speaking not only as a dog, but also on behalf of the entire Animal Kingdom as well as the Family of Plants, the Association of Insects and our Mother Earth, nurturer of us all. As I listened, I imagined Kanoe up on a stage before an audience. Apparently, since she'd been given the opportunity to speak, she intended to share what was on her mind and in her heart, so I settled in at my computer sensing I'd be there for awhile taking down her dissertation.

I began to realize the importance of her message to me and perhaps to other humans as well. It actually seemed as if she was speaking directly to me about specific issues I was trying to understand as a human. But at the same time, she was also speaking directly to her own human who was deeply moved by the message. The whole thing was kind of spooky and I still have those feelings whenever I think about it. It was one of those experiences that really blew me away and caused me to pause. I am delighted to be able to share Kanoe's message at last! You will meet her very soon!

What you hold in your hands and what follows is a collection of some of my most memorable conversations with dogs. It is with profound gratitude that I share with you the love, wisdom and patience of our dearest loyal and loving companion — the dog!

CHAPTER TWO

Dog Talk

I have the pleasure of meeting new dogs every day. People contact me to schedule phone appointments to talk with their dogs about many topics, including the dog's behavior, diet, health, transitions to new homes, or the transition of death. I rarely meet these dogs in person because I talk with so many pets from around the world, but we communicate in a way that is profound and memorable. When we've talked just once, we are forever connected and can talk again at any time. This particular type of communication is commonly referred to by humans as telepathy and I'd like to mention that the animals themselves often use the term "collective mind".

They say that when two or more beings of life consciously place their attention on conversing with one another in a manner of complete respect, patience and attentiveness as though nothing else exists in the world, they can join as one in collective mind. While we are in collective mind, we literally have opened ourselves to share who we are — our unique personalities, habits, tendencies, and experiences. To give you an example, I can be conversing with a dog and he or she will suddenly make a comment on an experience I had in my life or, while attempting to explain something to me, I'll hear, "You know how it was when you lived in the desert." Though we have never talked about me living in the desert, the dog has access to my experience of this because we have joined together as one during our conversation. When we join in collective mind all that we know and all that we are is available to be shared. So when I take a few moments to pause and get to know a dog I will learn many things about him or her and the dog in turn will learn many things about me. I literally feel their joy, sadness or pain. I will feel their personality and their likes and dislikes and they will feel mine.

I want to make an important point here that each of us humans has the ability to communicate with all the life around us in the way I have just described. I believe that it is a natural part of our genetic makeup. In working with clients and reminding them of their innate skills, I am constantly experiencing people discovering their natural abilities and feeling the passion of awakening a whole new life for themselves with the love and wisdom available to us all when we commune with Nature.

Historically, this manner of communication used to be common when we talked with one another as humans. In recent times, though, we have become a multitasking society where we are not very attentive or focused on any one thing, including our children, our parents, friends or even our dogs. I have had numerous dogs complain about their humans taking them for a walk while talking on their cell phone with someone else the entire time. We tend to think that being outside walking is spending "quality" time with our dog but in reality we're not really present with the dog nor are we present with the person we're talking with if we're on the phone!

A common suggestion from our dear friend the dog is that we humans take a few moments here and there during our day to practice doing just one thing and really focusing on that one activity or on that one conversation with our child, our spouse or our dog. They say that the magic of life truly resides in these moments of oneness with another living being and they highly recommend that we give ourselves moments of this pleasure. I encourage you to have some fun and experiment with this!

Another point I want to make is that, despite how busy we are in our lives, each one of us has experienced moments where we feel this magic of oneness and where we receive some insight from another source. It is almost impossible for us not to get some information from the life around us because we are constantly being bombarded by messages. For instance, you might have an aquarium that houses your pet gerbils. One day, although you are involved in an activity on the other side of the room, you suddenly find yourself standing near the aquarium looking in on the gerbils and the next thing you know, you're off to the kitchen to get them their favorite snack.

What was it that took you away from that project or television program and had you fetching food for your gerbils? Well, of course it was the gerbils! Animals are constantly broadcasting what they want us to do and oftentimes despite how busy our minds and bodies can be, we will suddenly pause and unknowingly respond to their requests. Another example is if you're driving, the thought to pick up some bones for your dog simply pops into your mind. Or, you suddenly have the idea to purchase a new food, or you have the thought to switch back to a food you'd fed your dog years ago. Where do these ideas come from? They come from your dog! After waiting patiently, your dog finally sensed that your mind had opened enough so his or her message could be heard and responded to! In general, we humans are very good at listening to our pets and naturally so — we love them and want them to feel our love in return and we want them to have vibrant health too!

Please keep this in mind: If you would like to hear your dog or the majestic tree outside the window or the grasshopper on the doorstep — YOU CAN! Each one of us has the ability to awaken our natural listening skills and when we really hear our dogs, we then have a greater appreciation for our lives and will share this joy with all those we meet, just like they do! They want us to feel the peace, pleasure and joy of simply being — just like a dog does!

The use of telepathic communication or collective mind allows me to converse with animals that live all around the world. When I am asked to talk with a dog, this is what I do: First, I pause and focus for a few moments on my breath so that I can let go of what I might have been thinking about or doing previously. Over the years, I have noticed that while I'm focusing on my breath, I have difficulty thinking about the past or the future, so this activity really brings me into the present and into the moment. Then when I feel quiet inside, I simply call out to the dog, usually in my head. I will say the dog's name and ask if he or she is available or willing to speak. Generally, most dogs are very excited and eager to converse. Occasionally I meet a dog who is shy and reserved but even with these dogs there is an eagerness to connect.

The purpose of my conversations is generally to evaluate and/or explain some kind of recent change in behavior with someone's dog, or to comfort an animal who is experiencing some health challenges. Or, there may be a change in the life of the human and some concern about how the dog is doing and questions about what he or she would prefer with these new circumstances. Whatever topics we focus on, I also like to ask the animal if they have anything else they would like to share with their human while they have this opportunity to express themselves in this way.

In the last thirteen years I have conversed with many dogs and have come to the conclusion that the primary focus for the majority of dogs is their human or humans. More specifically, it is the well-being of their people and people in general that is important to them, and this seems to be their favorite topic when they are communicating with me. It's not about gossip or sharing secrets about their humans, although I have had some humans say their dog was a tattle tale. Dogs often share suggestions as to how their people might think more lovingly of themselves or take better care of themselves. They often bring up particular hobbies or activities that they want their humans to get involved with. People are often surprised when they hear that their dog encourages them to go out and get some art supplies and take a water color class. It's not uncommon for me to hear people respond to their dog's wishes, saying that doing art has been a dream of theirs for years but that they'd never had time. Dogs will present ideas about how humans can make time for their dreams to blossom. They make recommendations with the hope that their people will find greater joy, fulfillment and peace on a daily basis. Dogs also give specific information for their human's health and well-being, including changes or additions to their diet, and sometimes they give me suggestions to enhance my well-being too.

People ask me how I receive the information. When I first meet a dog telepathically, I often feel a wave of joy wash over me in a powerful emotion. Sometimes if they're a little shy, the feelings are somewhat subdued. And if the animal is having health challenges, their responses may not be as strong as they might normally be. If they're not feeling well or if they're unhappy, I will feel that too. I receive the information in images, feelings, thoughts and even words and phrases. It is similar to how you might feel if you call a family member or close friend and before you even begin your conversation, you sense that he or she feels really happy or seems a little low. There are so many things that we naturally pick up when we connect with others, but because we don't often focus on these things, we tend to minimize our natural abilities to communicate telepathically. I just want to remind you once again that you *can* do this and I want to encourage you to take notice of what you sense in your daily life.

Getting back to my explanation, I often begin conversing with an animal by sitting down and opening a page on my computer and typing in my questions and the responses they give. The animals are generally so eager to share that they speak in an easy flow of conversation that I either type in or share with my client over the phone. Sometimes the animals give short answers and at other times, their answers can be quite lengthy — each animal is different, and just like people, some dogs are easier to talk with than others. I ask a lot of questions!

I probably talk with more dogs than any other animal in my daily conversations. As you can probably tell, they hold a warm place in my heart! When I have the opportunity, I like to open the floor, so to speak and open myself up to listen to as many dogs as possible in an afternoon. So rather than ask them questions from their humans, I like to listen to dogs who normally don't have the opportunity to talk to a human in this way. I enjoy simply asking them to share whatever they wish to say and then I just sit quietly and listen and record whatever they tell me. Sometimes I ask questions to encourage the animal to share their message and sometimes my curiosity gets the best of me and I want to ask a question. But, I try to just listen.

It was on one of these occasions that I gathered the following messages from a group of dogs who shared their stories, their wishes, their experiences and their concerns. These are dogs I had never met before and their humans had not asked me to talk with them. This was an open invitation for any dogs who wished to express themselves freely. In preparation to listen, I simply made a statement that I was available to listen to any dogs who wished to speak and I was instantly greeted by a dog who introduced himself as Doc.

In honor and gratitude for the love and dedication of our dear dogs, I present you with the stories these particular dogs shared with me on this day.

Go ahead, Doc! I am ready to record your message.

Hello, my name is Doc and I am a much-loved Basset Hound! Yes, I am adorable and fun loving. That is what I hear from my humans all the time and I believe it! I am here today to share some wisdom with my humans as well as any others who care to listen.

Oftentimes, humans will have certain standards for our care. It seems that the sense of fulfillment they could experience in living up to these standards is generally kept just out of reach. What I mean by this is that the human maintains the belief that they always fall short of the standards they have in their mind. They often feel that they are not doing enough or that what they are doing is incorrect. They can give us the most fabulous care, but think that they are falling short. It is like they never let themselves feel good about who they are, what they do and how wonderfully they care for us.

I mention this because it ultimately affects us, the animal. Most of us animals would agree that we love ourselves and have no shyness or self consciousness about expressing this. We love it when our humans love and honor themselves, too. Otherwise there is a constant battle going on in the mind and heart of the human as they fight with themselves, putting themselves down and never allowing themselves to fully feel the love and grati- tude we have to share because they don't believe they deserve our love. They don't believe that there is anything in them for us to feel grateful for.

When humans love themselves, they demonstrate this on a regular daily basis by saying "no" to things, people and activi- ties that drain them, even when it is us. They open themselves to feel our love fully and they are open to be filled, nurtured and fulfilled in their lives so they ultimately have an overflowing abundance of love to give. This is when we benefit most. It often means saying no to unrealistic requests or when the timing is not *right, etc. Saying no means saying "yes" to you, and it ultimately means saying yes to us. When you are at your best by allowing yourself to be loved and nurtured on a daily basis, you are also the best you can be for us. You are the best company and you are the healthiest, most vibrantly alive human you can be.*

Doc, will you give an example of what you mean?

Yes. My humans do not like to take me out walking in our neighborhood because for them, it does not feel like an inspiring place to walk. Most often, my colleagues and I go out through the doggie door whenever we wish and exercise on our own. My humans think that perhaps they are mistreating us by not taking us out into the neighborhood. But I too, find the neighborhood uninspiring and I do not have a desire to go walking there either. I love our home and I love the freedom to go in and out of the shelter whenever I wish. My colleagues concur!

My suggestion is that if you find yourself judging yourself with regard to the kind of care you are giving your pets, be realistic and ask yourself if you are simply looking for an excuse to beat yourself up or put yourself down. If you truly feel that there is a problem then check it out.

You humans quite often think it is all about you! You think you have done this wrong or that wrong. You think that we are unhappy having a little time on our own while you are away from the house or on vacation. We often feel delighted at the opportunity to have some peaceful time to ourselves. We also encourage vacations as we want to have new experiences too, and we often do this vicariously through you.

Don't think that you have to give it all up when you bring an animal companion into your life. Many of us want to go with you on your adventures. But when we cannot go with you, we like to go with you in spirit while keeping the home fires burning for your return. We often choose a human by how their lifestyle will match what we want for ourselves. Yes, usually we have chosen you!

We are opposed to one sacrificing their joy and passion for us or for anything else. You humans do this all the time in the name of us and others, but it is not really for us. If it was really for us, you would have to fill yourself with love and kindness first because that is the only way it can work. No, we see your sacrifice as that of a battle with your own being and it simply supports the battle you want to have with yourself. It gives you something to complain about; it gives you something to struggle with. It keeps you busy. You cannot find fulfillment or well-being for yourself through sacrifice of your own well-being. You must focus on you first and foremost. The more you do to be kind and nurturing to yourself, the more you do for us.

Humans find it more challenging to be kind to themselves than anything else. When you feel compassion for yourself, you experience profound changes at your core that align you with the sweetness of your true authentic self — God's Child. Then you are open to receive all the love and kindness that the universe has to offer. You become a magnet for receiving love and ease in life. Have you noticed that many of us animals already live in this loving consciousness of well-being? We exude peace and love. We love to embrace you with it. We are bursting with joy! That is how we are.

You too, will feel this when you open yourself to this love and *you too, will be bursting with it. Isn't this more purposeful and more helpful than being a martyr who sacrifices all the time, or being bitter and burned out? We don't ever wish to sacrifice our own and do not support this for our humans. We share from our abundance of love because we love ourselves. Therefore, we are open to receive it and we have an abundance of love to give. We want you to continue on your journey feeling your path beneath you, just as we do. If it means that we require a different situation or experience, we will go one way or another. If it means that you must move or change in a manner that separates us, so be it! We encourage you to go, to follow your path because when one commits to something or someone that no longer works, to stay is to lose one's aliveness. Of course there is value in staying long enough to consider it all, including one's responsibility and being able to feel one's true path, but that is all.*

Doc, what do you mean by that last part about staying and leaving?

What I am saying is that there may be times where we are separated by vacations or necessary adventures and that sometimes we simply must part and go our separate ways. The main thing we dogs suggest is that our humans be completely honest with themselves and that they live honestly in love and compassion for themselves. In this way they are also living in love and compassion for us and for all life. Our humans often make sacrifice after sacrifice of their true spirit to the point where they barely feel any passion for life at all. They live in their own prison of quiet turmoil. We suggest they open their hearts to their own dear selves by beginning a dialog with themselves. For instance, they might begin to ask themselves how they are doing and what they can do personally to open themselves to more joy in their lives. They can ask themselves how they feel about this and that. They can pay attention to what has them feeling most alive. They can choose and they can ponder and hopefully, they can take action on their unfulfilled dreams. In opening their hearts to themselves, they will most naturally have opened their hearts to all life, including of course their dear dogs!

Thanks Doc!

As Doc finished sharing, I felt the presence of another dog waiting and ready to speak so I gave this new dog the go ahead to begin as soon as Doc finished.

OK, now I'm going to leave you to the dogs!

My name is Mystic and I am a dog. I look like a rag dog with wiry hair and a style all my own! I have quite a following of fans — you'd think I was famous! I have a fabulous human who is well-liked by many other humans. We socialize a lot, and every day is an adventure. I am friends with all my human's friends and there are dog friends as well. I feel such gratitude for my life! Yeah! It is so much fun!

I want to share my mission and yes, of course I have a mission! It is my goal to meet and greet as many humans as possible to impart a little of my magic and wisdom. Those who know me recognize something magical about me. They like to be around me and have an opportunity to look into my magic. I literally glow like a person who is feeling blissful. I feel this way all the time and I so want to share it with all the humans I meet, but I am not overly assertive in making myself known. I am friendly, but a little reserved out of respect for the humans. I don't like to overpower them with kisses or jump on them — you will not see me behave in this way. I like to just be and to consciously invite the humans to come close. We move close slowly and respectfully. Sometimes in their excitement to meet me, young humans will run up enthusiastically. I don't have any problems with this at all! I love the young humans and have lots of fun with them. Thank you for allowing me to share! All my love and blessings to you humans!

Hello, my name is Bridgett! I am delighted to have this opportunity to talk with you humans! I would like to share some insights that I believe could be helpful to humans near and far. First, let me say that I am a dog. I know a description is important to you humans so let me say that I am white with hair that is mostly short, but I do have some long pieces and some curls at the end of the hairs. I have dark brown eyes and a cold black nose. No other colors, no other markings. I am white, but I am beautiful and usually I am really a bright white color because I like to be clean. I am about the size of a small coyote with fine, feminine bones.

OK, let me get on with what I came to say. It has come to my attention that my humans feel guilty when they are really busy and they think there is little time to walk me or just to relax together in the evening. I really don't like to feel my humans feeling even more distress about these things when they are already feeling overwhelmed with their responsibilities. The last thing I want is to be a stress to my family!

I suggest that my family and perhaps other human families as well do what they can to take care of themselves to avoid these states of overwhelm and stress. But when it is unavoidable, I encourage them to put their energy and focus into bringing themselves back into balance by getting plenty of rest, doing something fun to remind them of what life is all about or whatever is necessary to bring themselves back into balance as soon as possible. Sometimes the best thing you can do is to take me for a walk or to just be with me. I will accompany you in your rest and in your play, and I will help remind you of the important things. Please don't feel bad about missing some walks or being really busy! You only make it worse. You cause more stress for yourselves and you take yourself farther away from bringing yourselves back into balance. Be kind to yourselves and you will feel good soon! Thank you for listening! I love you!

Hello my name is Winston, Winnie the Pooh dog that is! I am a yellow dog with big ears! Some people think I look silly and have the thought that if the wind picked up, I would fly. I am a really good companion — a steady, loving dog who is always there for my humans.

I want to say a little something about the human tendency to want a dog of "fine" breeding and/or training. If you really have your heart set on a certain breed, look or characteristic, I support you in fulfilling this dream. But if you are really open in your choice of a companion, I would encourage you to consider a blend of a few or many breeds. We can be remarkable characters with brilliance and style. I might not have the elegance or beauty of a "purebred" dog, but I have the intelligence, personal-

30

ity, and sense of humor to handle any situation.

I never needed any "training"; I just knew what to do and my humans and I live a life of joy and compatibility that never ceases to amaze them. They can take me anywhere; we meet all sorts of dogs and people and I am always a delight to be with. They can turn me loose and know that I will get along well with anyone, that I won't run off even if I am in a new place and they know that I will not go out into the road. I am wise and loving and a joy to all who know me. I know how to live and I am the "little Buddha" of the family! They don't realize this, but I can share it with you!

Hello, my name is Sam. I am a girl dog. Sometimes humans are not sure if I am a girl dog or a boy dog. My name can go either way. I really don't care! I am not in any way offended by being called "he", or a boy dog. I think humans can relax about these things as well. I don't know why it is so important to be a "man" or a "woman", but I guess that is why I am a dog!

My name is Samuel, and I am a boy dog! I want to share a few things with you today. First, let me say that I am a purebred Schnauzer with fine features and pleasing characteristics. I also have great intelligence. You might think that I am bragging, but I believe these things to be true and I am comfortable in saying this. I would love it if my humans would pay more attention to their fine qualities and celebrate them. It seems that humans like to hide them and focus more on what they think of as their weaknesses or things they do not like. But let me get back to what I really wanted to share.

I want to say that I do not like to travel. I feel sick whenever

I am anywhere near a car. I don't like the movement and I don't like the way my stomach feels. Luckily my humans are homebodies! They really enjoy being at home and don't feel the desire to travel much. When they do, they take me to a kennel. I would prefer to be home but I would rather be at a kennel than traveling about. I think I am unusual for my breed and it never worked out for me to be a show dog because of this. I have a really good life! I love my humans!

Hello, my name is Peter. I am a Doberman dog. My family dearly loved me. They took me everywhere when I was a pup and tried to do the same when I was an adult. But I began to be increasingly protective to the point of snapping at their friends and once I even snapped at their new baby and showed my teeth. My people were very sad, confused and worried about what to do with me. In considering my behavior, it was dangerous to have me near the baby. It was dangerous to have me around their friends, and finding another home posed the danger of someone else getting hurt. In the end it was decided to put me to sleep. I know this was an agonizing decision for my people but I agreed with it. The last thing I wanted was to hurt anyone, but sometimes our genetics as dogs can get out of hand. I am not talking about my breed. We are sensitive dogs and quite lovable and safe, but my particular genes were inbred so much that I was having some serious difficulties in keeping myself sane. I have no hard feelings toward my people. They did what was best for me and what was best for all. I would like to express my wish to breeders to be very careful in what you do. Give more thought to creating wonderful temperaments and healthy dogs *mentally and physically and less to our shape, our size, or our color. That is all!*

By the way, as we have just experienced with Peter, telepathic communication gives us a way to talk with both animals and people who have made the transition of death. Usually if the animal doesn't let on that they're "dead" I might not know it because they can feel as vibrantly alive as ever. When I talk with lost pets, the first question I usually ask is whether they are alive and well in the body known to their humans. I learned the hard way that just because they seem alive doesn't mean that they are alive in their body. For instance, a dog might be talking very excitedly about an experience they had and then later in the conversation tell you about their death. OK, enough from me — let me turn you over to the dogs once again!

Hello, my name is Wilma! I am a dog. I am short and furry, not fluffy! My hair is straight and it is white and bushy and playful. I am a delight to my humans. I love life and I love to smile and glow!

Thank you for your wonderful presence, Wilma! I feel your joy and delight — it is contagious! Do you have something you would like to share?

Yes, I want to share some basic insights into the world of animals. We are quite similar to humans in that each individual dog or cat or horse or iguana is unique in its history and experience. Each one of us has a dream and a purpose. We have things we want to learn and things we want to experience. We choose our humans based on what we want for ourselves. Sometimes we might make what seems like a mistake. Sometimes other humans may find our situation unbearable and they may rescue us. Sometimes we are ready to be rescued because we have experienced enough. I have had many adventures! I chose a lovely couple of humans this time. They are content and peaceful. I am enjoying this very much because it really matches how I feel. We are very compatible. At other times, I have chosen humans and situations that were not so peaceful. My experiences have me appreciating this adventure more than I ever would have.

Thank you, Wilma! Do you have anything else you wish to say?

No, I will let another speak.

My name is Dizzy and I am a dog. Yes, I am silly and playful, but I have wisdom to share! I love my life! I love my humans, but I don't like my name! I literally feel dizzy because any connotation of this word is floating in the consciousness of the humans who know me and those that I meet. The name may seem to fit, but it really has me spinning. I ask for a new name, one that matches my aspirations, things I know I can achieve. I know I am spacey and silly, but I also wish to honor my wise and stable side. Yes, I have aspects of me like this — I really do! I am seeking balance in myself and would find it helpful if my humans would consider giving me a new name— something expansive, something that gives me more freedom to be my unique self.

Do you have any suggestions?

Yes, I like the name Dan. It is kind and soft, but also leaves it up to me to be me.

Thank you for sharing, Dan! I don't know your humans, but I will pass this along to others so that they will give consideration to what you have said in naming their pets. And, I will think of you as Dan!

Thank you! This makes me feel good!

My name is Silvi. I love my life and my humans! I want to say that these are not my first humans. I have had a few other homes. I want to express my gratitude to the humans in my past for having the courage and insight to let me go so that I could ultimately join my present human family. It was OK where I was before. They were fairly happy and so was I, but we all knew that there was another dog who was a better match for the activity and lifestyle of my first humans. I was content, but I really wanted something else, a different experience and relationship as well. Had my humans been steadfast in thinking they had to keep me forever because they made that commitment, I would not have found my fabulous home and the profound connection I now have with these humans. We would have all settled for a lesser experience and given up the fulfillment of our dreams.

I am here to encourage people not to settle for what does not work. I encourage humans to seek an ideal relationship with their pets and that if this does not work for them, to be open and willing to let us go so that we too, can find our dream and our precious place.

My name is Frederic. I am a Chihuahua-Shih Tzu dog cross. I think I might have a little poodle in me too! I am adorable and I know it! I really enjoy barking at the big dogs! I am not afraid of anyone! I also love to be the center of attention.

My humans take care of everything for me. I like to work them for every detail. I love them and they listen to all of my requests. They take care of me like I am their baby. Sometimes I feel their frustration at my never-ending requests and needs. I am like a baby who never grows up, who never takes responsibility for my own life. This can be good and it can be desired by humans, but it can also be a continual stress and something that takes away from the true delight and joy of my humans.

I like to push and push for more and more, not out of a dislike for my humans but, on the contrary, out of love. You see, it is my distinct desire to push and push and push so that they will see how they continually sacrifice their own well-being and needs for the good of another, and how this is a continual drain of their energy because they're not taking the best care of themselves. It is my greatest wish that one day they will put their foot down as you humans say, and value themselves like no other. It is my hope that they will decide to make their well-being number one so they can take the best care of both themselves and me. This will ultimately have them feeling fulfilled and nourished by their human experience. It will have them feeling delight and passion in the simplicity of a breath and of a moment, and gratitude beyond measure for their friends, family, experiences and for me.

You see, I can push and push and they can sacrifice themselves over and over again, but they really have little to give in comparison to when they are fulfilled. When they are fulfilled, they feel the love of God flowing to and through them. They feel the abundance of this love and they take good care of them-

selves by being open to receive love. When they receive this love, they are overflowing with it and it goes out to me and all other life around them. When they are not open to receiving this love, they are willing to sacrifice their safety, their sanity, their joy, their rest and their health for another. And this rarely helps the other.

Look at me, for example. I am a spoiled brat! I don't need all this lavishness and pampering! I could really do with some experience as a real dog. I think this would be satisfying to me. I want to get my paws dirty! I want to roll in the dirt! I want to play with other dogs and I don't mind being pushed around a little. I am really cocky! I could use a little reality check! Do you get what I'm saying here?

I believe I do. Thank you, Frederic! And thanks to all of you who have shared your messages today!

This gives you an idea of the kind of conversations you can have in a short period of time with dogs you don't even know! Well, actually I have to admit that I do know "Winnie the Pooh Dog" who simply showed up in my awareness just like the others and began talking. I recognized him, but allowed him to continue because I knew he had something important to share. I wouldn't want to stop a dog from sharing his message! You never know who might appear, but the depth of their sharing can be profound and touching. I encourage you to pause one afternoon and invite a few dogs to share their love and wisdom. We humans have kept company with dogs for approximately 14,000 years, and it's amazing that despite all the changes we've made in our lives, dogs continue to be highly attuned and connected to us.

DOGS SAY THE DARNDEST THINGS

They really know — and are concerned about — what's going on with us! And they also seem to know what would help us most to experience the kind of peacefulness and joy they experience in just

CHAPTER THREE
Henry

L ast week, I received a call from a woman named Sarah who
had some questions that were weighing heavily on her
mind about her dog, Henry. We made an appointment for
me to talk with him a few days later. Sarah loved her dog dearly
and was concerned about his level of contentment. Sometimes
Henry looked sad to her when she was petting the other animals
they lived with. Sarah believed Henry was jealous of her other
pets and that he was unhappy when she gave them her attention. In addition to her concerns about Henry's happiness, Sarah
wanted to feel more confident in her communications with her
dog. I suggested that we ask Henry and her other pets for specif-
ics as to how she might enhance her communication skills. I've
learned over the years that animals know their humans better than
anyone so I like to ask them directly for their assistance.

I took a few slow, deep breaths in preparation to talk with
Henry.

Hello, Henry!

Hello, Woman!

Will you tell me about yourself and share some information to clear up questions that your woman has for you?

Yes, of course! I am a big black dog — not just tall but also big! I look like a big brute, but I can assure you that I am quite safe and gentle! I would be pleased to answer my woman's questions. I think I have her puzzled! This is good! I say this is good because when one is puzzled, they seek to find the truth and in this, there is openness for receiving new information or for a new and even more magical experience of life.

I love my dear woman and my dear man. He seems to be comfortable with our relationship at the moment. She questions some things. Perhaps you will let me go ahead and share with her and then if there are questions, we can address them. Is this acceptable to you, Woman?

Yes, of course! Please go ahead Henry!

OK, this is to my woman. I am here to show you a different image. I am not your average dog, and I respond in ways that have you wondering. This is good because the more you hear from the life around you, the more surprised you will be. Things are quite different than what you humans think of as the truth. For instance, you believe that I am jealous of the attention given to the other dogs and the cats. This is not true. I actually love seeing and feeling them being loved! It brings a smile to my face! I look over at you loving them and I smile; meanwhile, you think I am sad and that I want all of your love. I already feel I have all

40

of your love because of the way that I know you feel about me.

My presence with you may bring up questions to assist you in increasing your awareness to all that is. I have heard you say, "Your eyes are so expressive! Why can't I hear what you're telling me?"

My response to you, my dear human, is that you can hear me. All that is required is that you listen. When I say "listen," I truly mean just that. I mean that you stop the chatter in your mind when another being is talking so that you can listen, truly listen. Free your mind of any assumptions about what you think we are thinking, and instead quiet your wonderful self to hear what it is that we have to say.

Whatever is done to improve human communication especially in the realm of listening, will probably help in communicating with us as well. The one suggestion I have is that I would recommend you not look into my eyes when you want to listen (at least initially), and that you have me outside and you inside, or me here and you somewhere else.

You are distracted by my physicality, dear Woman. Humans have put great effort into studying animal behavior by watching our movements and expressions and analyzing them based on how you would analyze a fellow human. We suggest that you not analyze us in this way and that instead you situate yourself in a place away from us and that you focus your attention on listening.

Woman (Maia), do you have any personal information you can share with my human that would help in this regard?

I do! When I first started working with clients, they wanted me to meet their animals in person and had great difficulty understanding how I could communicate with animals without knowing or seeing them. All I asked for was the name of the animal and what kind of animal it was, and that is usually all I ask for today as well. Sometimes local clients would insist that I meet their animal, but I preferred to do so after I had already communicated with them. I love meeting animals in person and I receive many photos after our conversations, but I feel most clear when I commune with them without their physical presence. I agree with you, Henry, that we humans depend on our physical senses so much that we often feel lost without the opportunity to assess a situation without them.

When I work with students reminding them of their natural animal communication skills, I frequently must ask them to set aside their assumptions, beliefs, preconceived notions and concerns about their pet so that they can truly hear him or her. It is much like listening to another human. If we think we know everything about them based on our observations, we may have difficulty hearing anything other than what we think we already know. Students can converse with an animal they have never seen before with great ease, but may at first have difficulty conversing with their own pet because they have already decided how their pet feels, what it thinks and what it wants. When they open themselves to truly listen, students are often amazed to find out that their pet has different views on many things.

For instance, Henry, your woman was convinced that you were jealous when she petted the other dogs and because of that, she altered her manner of interacting with all of you based on this belief. It will be a surprise for her to read your message that in fact, you are not jealous at all, but that you are looking intently at her, giving love to the others because you enjoy seeing this. And, she might be surprised to hear that you feel very secure in her love for you. As my horse friend Delight says, entire relationships between humans and animals can be based on a belief that is untrue. When we set aside our beliefs and assumptions about what an animal thinks or feels we have an opportunity to truly hear the animal, and get to know him or her in a profound way.

Thank you for sharing this, Woman! Let me continue with this information for my human. OK, so what I ask, my dear human, is that when you wish to communicate with me, go to another place — to work, to a café or some other place. Another option is that you can put me outside and make yourself comfortable in the home. I do not want you to have me in your physical presence because at the moment, it is too much of a distraction for you.

Have a notebook handy. Think of me and I will be there with you in thought. Just think of my name and see what you feel. I will send you messages. Then ask me some simple questions like, "Henry, are you happy?" Notice what you feel inside yourself and write down any words, images or thoughts you have.

Once you feel that loving connection with me, allow yourself to write whatever seems to pop into your mind. Please do not judge what you write or even think about it — just allow it to flow. And do not worry about where it is coming from, just write!

It is good to free up your inhibitions on this. You are trying too hard, because you have expectations. Be in the present and do this for yourself, for your own enjoyment. Let go of any ex-

pectations you might have and just focus on what you are doing when you are doing it. Allow the future to unfold. You will truly feel the magic if you allow it to spontaneously occur. Take it as a loving adventure into the awareness of the life around you and of your own dear self.

Sarah thanked me, thanked Henry and promised to follow his advice.

CHAPTER FOUR

Ben

It was mid afternoon and the culmination of a busy day of conversing with animals and their humans. I headed out to meet a friend to do some exploring in the high desert of central Oregon. The vistas were spectacular with the Cascade Mountain range to our immediate west and the sun gently setting down on Pine Mountain to the east.

Walking in this magic land has always inspired me, and I returned to the house feeling refreshed and rejuvenated. I decided to check my emails one last time before settling in for the evening.

The first message I read came from Susan, from the Midwest. Susan asked me to talk with her dog, Ben. Ben was having difficulty standing up and seemed to be in pain in various places along his spine. Numerous tests had been performed at the vet clinic, but Ben's condition continued to be a mystery. I adjusted my schedule for the following morning so that I could talk with Ben as I felt the urgency of the situation. From what Susan shared, I gathered that Ben was in some discomfort. I was eager to ask him if there was something his human could do to help him feel better.

After conversing with a number of animals from around the world earlier that morning, I settled in to talk with Ben. I took a few minutes to quiet myself and clear my mind in preparation to meet him. When I felt ready, I greeted the dog by saying hello just like I would greet a human. But in the case of the animals, I say hello in my head. I said, "Hello Ben" and I immediately heard the reply:

Hello Woman!

Ben, I would like to get to know you and ask you all about yourself, but I feel a sense of urgency in regard to the pain you may be feeling. I suggest that we get right to the point and talk about how you are feeling, what is causing your symptoms, and what your woman may do to help you. Are you agreeable to that?

No, no I am not agreeable to that! I want you to feel my energy; let's have a proper dog/human greeting!

OK, thanks Ben! Let me quiet myself and set aside the concerns and sense of urgency that I was feeling.

I closed my eyes for a few moments, breathed slowly and deeply. Once again I joined Ben, but this time I was ready to take my time and get acquainted.

OK Ben, I feel you now! I have a big smile on my face! I have such a loving feeling in my heart and I also feel your jolly, easy-going nature. I see and feel you snooping around. You often have your nose to the ground. Is that correct?

BEN

Yes it is! Welcome to my world! Let me see what I pick up from you, Woman. I feel this unquestionable sweetness! And you really love to live. You are playful too, but also serious and concerned.

Sounds familiar!

It is a great pleasure to meet you, Woman!

It is a great pleasure to meet you too, Ben!

Go ahead with your questions, Woman.

Ben, your human is concerned about you. She told me that sometimes you cannot walk. From her observations, you have swelling around your shoulders and you have pain if she touches your low back. As you know, there have been many examinations performed on you and no one seems to really understand what is causing your discomfort. There is no evidence of arthritis or disc problems from the X-rays taken. She also indicated that you were having difficulty standing up at times and that you seemed to have some weakness in your spine, hips and hind legs.

This is true!

She also said that she thinks that you respond well to prednisone and painkillers. Ben, how do you feel at this moment?

I hurt.

Where do you hurt?

I feel pain in my head, around my eyes and in the back of my head behind my ears.

What is the pain like?

It isn't always there but it is there often. It hurts in other places too, in my back and shoulders — everything tightens up.

Ben, do you know what is causing this pain?

Before Ben could even begin to answer my question, I was overcome by a profound sense of grief. If I hadn't been sitting down I would have dropped to my knees at the intensity of the emotion. It took a few moments and a few breaths to bring myself back to address Ben.

Ben, I am feeling immense sadness. I have tears coming to my eyes and running down my face. Is this sadness a result of your painful condition, or is it related to the cause of your condition, or something else?

There is sadness that is not totally being expressed. I am carrying it in my body. The expression of this sadness will lighten me.

Is this your sadness, Ben?

No.

Ben, your woman mentioned that your friend died. She wondered if you might be sad about the loss of your companion dog. Is this true?

No, I am not sad about her. We communicate all the time!
The physical challenges I am facing will not be seen in normal diagnostic manners.

Ben, you say you carry this sadness in your body, and that this is causing your pain and discomfort. Why did you take on these emotions?

Because I wanted to assist the child; she could not carry it all and continue as she was for she was not working with her feelings. I gave her a reprieve, as it were.

Ben, who is this child?

I prefer not to say at this time. It is not important that you know the identity. Please be patient with me in this. As the sadness begins to be addressed by her, the pressure will release within me. The more the child opens to her emotional state of being the better I will feel.

Please give more information about how to help you, Ben.

First it is important for the child to address the sadness, to bring it out in the open so that she may heal. She may share the sadness, express it, allow it to be felt and acknowledged until she is full of it. Then she may release it and move on.

My muscles will begin to relax once the child opens up. As the child begins to release the sadness, it would help to have chiropractic treatment and massage to assist my body in moving out these emotions which I agreed to carry. My woman may learn to massage me.

Natural pain relief and anti-inflammatory products from the plant kingdom are preferable to any other medicine and may be helpful in keeping me comfortable while my body releases the sadness.

49

VERY IMPORTANT! For all the humans in my life, and especially for my human: hold me in your thoughts as running, playing and wagging my tail.

Keep the picture of what you want in your thoughts and dismiss any negative pictures or thoughts as they enter your mind. Replace any negative pictures or thoughts immediately with thoughts of me running, playing and wagging my tail.

This and the release of the sadness in the child are the two most important things to bring me to the vibrantly healthy state you desire.

It is important to note that if the sadness is not released from the child, I will continue to hold the emotion no matter what treatment I receive. If the child chooses not to release the sadness that is OK; I will continue to carry it even if it causes me to cross over. I do this lovingly and have no fear of leaving this body.

Ben, thank you for answering my questions. I will share this information with your human.

Thank you, Woman!

I sent this dialogue to Susan and received the following reply.

Maia,

Thank you so much for the information. It was very accurate. Ben and I have always been deeply connected. I have never seen an animal respond so much to my emotions!! He pays attention to every sound I make and gets very depressed if I am sad.

As you probably guessed, the child he was talking about

was me. I have gone through some rough times and I know Ben was aware of it. Things have improved greatly but I have a long way to go.

The information you have given me has already become life-changing. I never thought that Ben's pain could actually be mine and I never really recognized how much sadness I'm still holding on to.

Ben has already responded to massage. It was very evident that it made him feel more relaxed and comfortable. Ben and I will work through this together and we will become healthy and strong.

I now realize that I can't waste one more day pretending nothing is wrong. Every day I will work at improving my life, not only for myself but also for Ben. I owe him that!!!

Maia, I need him to know how deeply touched I am that he would go through such physical pain to lessen my emotional pain. More importantly, I need him to know that he no longer has to do this because things will improve. I don't want anything to happen to Ben and it scared me that he would be willing to shoulder my pain, even if it cost him his life. He is such an amazing animal and I hope he knows how grateful I am for his love and loyalty.

Thank you, Maia!
Susan.

After receiving this message I reconnected with Ben.

Ben, do you have anything else you would like to tell your woman?

Please love your dear self! Nothing would bring me more joy than for you to realize what a wonderful human you are and to see you treat yourself based on this understanding. You deserve to be treated with great love and respect by you, and those you choose to have around you.

I love you so much and I feel so delighted to have you as my human!

I passed along Ben's message to Susan by email. It was nearly a year before I heard from her again. She sent me this note.

Maia,

I want you to know that in a matter of one week, my positive images of Ben running the wide open green fields without pain, tail wagging, brought him from a state of not being able to function at times to being almost entirely pain free.

He has only had one episode of slight pain in his back and that was a couple months after his dramatic improvement. It has almost been a year and that was the last episode of pain in his back he has had. In fact, HE PLAYS TUG-OF-WAR WITH THE ROPE TOYS NOW!!! I could never get him to play before!

In my opinion, these changes were only due to the change in how I viewed his ailments, and by being happy and positive in the household. This has done more for the health of my dogs and me than any conventional medicine ever has. Conventional medicine will always be a part of their care. We can never lose sight of the lives that the medical profession saves on a daily basis! I have a wonderful vet clinic that

BEN

takes outstanding care of my precious ones. I am thankful for them every day for many conditions they have helped me out with for our family dogs.

Thanks again Maia!
Susan

I decided to talk with Ben again to see if he had anything he wished to express. I sat quietly as usual, took a few relaxing breaths and invited Ben to speak.

Ben, do you have anything else you would like to say? Would you be willing to describe yourself?

Yes, of course! You might have already guessed that I am a loving sort! Oh, and I am a dog! I think I am about medium size and build. I am very solid in myself and very, very jolly! I love life! I love my companions and I love my woman!

I would also like to mention that my story is not that unusual — in fact, it is quite common. I would encourage humans to check in with themselves on a regular basis to be sure that they are dealing with whatever frustrations or sadness they have. If they are constantly making adjustments to be aware of how they feel, and they are making adjustments responsibly to bring greater peace and joy, they probably are not carrying many unresolved challenges. Challenges can be arguments within oneself, lack of forgiveness or arguments with another. They can also be a belief that they are a victim of injustice.

The important thing is to face whatever it is and to work lovingly with oneself on the situation. Whenever you notice your animal being less than normal, you might ask yourself how you are doing. The solution is often in that question.

When humans maintain challenges within themselves with-out resolution, they create imbalances in the body over time. The energy must reside somewhere and if they hold it unresolved, it will reside in their physical body and quite often in ours.

As stated before, I agreed to carry the emotion of sadness. I was not a victim of my woman. She is my loving companion and I adore her!

CHAPTER FIVE
Shane

I enjoyed talking with Roberta and her Golden Retriever, Shane, a number of times over the last three years. Our conversations began when Roberta was in the process of moving and needed to put Shane in a kennel for a period of time that was a little longer than her normal vacation. She was concerned about boarding him and wanted to be sure that Shane understood that it was temporary and that she would visit him daily until they were once again living together. Shane was a very understanding dog and shared information to help Roberta calm herself through their transition. After being settled in their new home for nearly a year, Roberta called me because Shane had begun to have seizures. I began a series of questions to find out what was causing them.

Hello Shane, how are you feeling?

Great!

Do you feel any pain anywhere?

No, I feel a little yucky in my digestion, but I have no pain.

Shane, do you know why you are having seizures? Is this connected to how you are feeling with your digestion?

Yes, I know why and it is connected. I am a very sensitive dog. Some of the food that I am eating now makes me feel yucky. It is the oils; they are old and stale. It is also the grains that are unnatural in a common diet for my kind. And then there are the things I cannot identify that have me wanting to eat more of the food to find out what it is, but ultimately have me feeling bad. This is what is causing my seizures. I am literally sick of my food! My body is doing the best it can to deal with it. It keeps going, but I don't have the vibrant health I love because of how the food I eat taxes my cells.

Shane, would you explain what you mean by "the grains that are unnatural as a common diet for my kind"?

I am a dog! Dogs do not normally eat grains like wheat and corn. I eat grass once in a while as a digestive aid, but it is un-natural and unhealthy for a dog to eat like a horse.

Thank you! Would you further explain what you mean by "things I cannot identify"?

I can only say that there are things in my food that are not really nutritious, but that make a dog want to eat the food. After I finish, I wonder why I finished it, much like a human would wonder why they finished a meal that tasted bad. For me and from what I have heard, it is a daily occurrence for many dogs to feel this way.

SHANE

When you say that you have heard from other dogs, how do you communicate? Where do you get this information?

We talk when we meet in person, much like you humans do. Not in barking. We talk in the way you and I are talking right now. Someone could walk by your computer and have no idea that you are talking with a dog and typing in our conversation as we go along. We dogs talk to each other as neighbors, but we also can talk with our friends all over the planet. We have quite a network, but we tend to stay local. We really like to meet in person when we can.

Shane, how can your human help you feel your most vibrant self?

Yeah! I like this topic! I need a new food. Let me give you some ideas that would make me really happy. I want to eat a raw food diet at least two to three times a week. My woman can explore makers of raw dog food diets in the area or bring the food in from somewhere else. Otherwise I would like to eat cooked food, like meat and veggies. A little rice is OK or plain yogurt. She can find some healthy products that are natural and fresh without any strange ingredients, and without wheat, corn or rancid oils, too. I ask that she give me organic foods, to avoid feeding me chemicals from the vegetables, and growth hormones from the meat. She can give me a mixture of natural, organic foods and I will be thrilled! My vibrant health will return and I will have no more seizures.

Shane, I receive an increasing number of requests for raw and/or home-cooked diets from the dogs and cats I converse with. Why is this? Also, will you explain why you request organic vegetables and meats?

The food we have been eating is not good for us! It is old, strange, and it causes us to lose our vitality. It literally poisons many of us. It is like humans eating a food that they have negative reactions to, but yet they continue to eat it. These pet foods I am referring to cause sluggish digestion, bloating, itching, scratching, scaly skin and lethargy. Many of these old foods contain the lowest quality ingredients, and there is little control over what goes into our food. We animals are speaking out and feel fortunate to have this opportunity!

The reason I request organic vegetables is because they have little or no poisonous chemicals in them. Regularly available meats and milk usually contain growth hormones and other chemicals that cause much of the disease in animals today. If you look at the rate of disease in pets today as opposed to even twenty years ago, there is a significant increase due to the toxicity of our foods. We encourage our humans to eat the healthiest foods, too!

Thank you, Shane, is there anything else you would like to share with your woman?

Please tell her that I adore her!

Shortly after this conversation, Roberta sent me a message indicating that Shane was on a new diet and had had no seizures for two months. She was very excited, and told me that he was now looking bright, happy and healthy!

Six months passed with no seizures and then I got a call from

SHANE

Roberta who said that the day before, Shane had two seizures, one in the morning and one in the evening. I set aside time right away to get in touch with him to find out what was going on.

Shane, how are you feeling?

Stressed!

What is stressing you, Shane? Is it something to do with your food?

My stress is unrelated to my food. I like my food now! My stress is my concern for my woman. Her stress is my stress — we are one!

Is this financial stress?

No, no more stress than usual.

Does this have to do with her career?

No, it has to do with a man.

Is she still involved with this man?

Yes.

Is this a healthy relationship for her?

No!

Why?

He is self-centered, bossy, controlling, and he has her stressed, thin and running all the time.

Does he like you?

No. He has thought of eventually doing away with me,
but this is not my main concern. I worry for her.

After talking with Shane I called Roberta to share this information. She responded, "Maia, I am really surprised at what
Shane shared with you! I thought this was about Shane, not me!
I had no idea that my stuff would affect him this way. What he
has shared with you is true. The man he described is currently out
of town and I have had a chance to gain a greater understanding
of our relationship while he has been away. He really is selfish!
For instance, when I hurt my back and was resting, he never even
called. There are many examples. It is also interesting that he has
suggested that I give Shane away on numerous occasions. I never
felt comfortable leaving Shane with him. Now I know why!
Please tell Shane thank you! I love him so much!"

I said, "Roberta, Shane would like to add a few things. He
would like you to allow yourself to examine all the things that
make this relationship unacceptable to you. You have a tendency
to make up for others' shortcomings and not really acknowledge
them. He wants you to allow yourself to feel your true frustration
at being treated poorly so that you will feel comfortable in letting
this man go."

"Shane also indicates that he feels the man returning and
that he is again concerned for you. He asks you to open yourself
to a person who feels your joy is their joy. Basically a person who
loves you so much that he loves seeing you happy and doing
things that he knows you love. He says that this man falls short
in this area and is threatened by your happiness, as it takes the
focus off him. Also, Shane wants you to open yourself to a man

who truly is available to you. Shane says he will be your man for now and that when your true partner arrives he will share you with him. Shane will let you know what he thinks when you meet him."

After pausing thoughtfully for a moment, Roberta said, "Maia, it is true! Whenever I have been really excited about something he has showed little interest and almost seemed irritated by my joy. Shane is such a wise dog! Thank you, Shane and thank you, Maia!"

Thank you, Roberta and Shane!

CHAPTER SIX
Mash Unit Dogs

In the late nineties I traveled to the Galapagos Islands to fulfill a dream that had been awakened in me years before when I was in junior high school. I still remember watching a video of the unique species of animals from the Islands in class. As a young teenager I wanted to visit the Galapagos and see the amazing animals that lived there. When my life finally took me to the Islands on a vacation as an adult, I discovered that they were more magical than I had dreamed. One day on the Island of Floreana I was sitting on a log on a small stretch of beach. The grains of sand appeared to be tiny polished gem stones courting translucent turquoise waters. The rest of the small group of tourists was a little way off in the distance. I suddenly felt a powerful emotion well up in me and knew that this was just the beginning of my getting to know the Galapagos. Although this 8-day cruise was amazing, I knew without a doubt that I was destined to be here longer for reasons I was not aware of at the time. Sure enough, within two months I was miraculously back in the Islands and I lived there for two years, from 1999 through 2001, finally returning to the U.S. in April of 2002 after spending some time exploring in the Andes Mountain regions and the Amazon Rain Forest. During my time on the Islands, I became a volunteer for the Galapagos National Park and several international organizations which were doing work to assist the Park in the protection of rare and endangered species on the land and in the marine reserve.

While on a visit to San Francisco in 2000 to update my visa, I visited the headquarters of one of the organizations I had been working for in the Islands. There I had the pleasure of meeting Emma Clifford who, in addition to her work with this particular group, had for years worked with feral cats in San Francisco. Emma was making plans to launch a new organization called Animal Balance whose purpose was to fund, organize and operate spay and neuter campaigns in areas of the world that were being threatened by people's pets that had become feral. Initially, Animal Balance's primary focus would be the Galapagos Islands where feral cats and dogs were endangering the unique indigenous species of animals there who were often found living nowhere else on the Earth.

That first meeting with Emma began an association that continues to this day. I became a member of the Board of Directors for Animal Balance and helped in the early preparations by sharing the names of people I knew in the villages and offering suggestions on how to get to know and work with these natives for the initial spay and neuter campaigns in the Islands.

Emma and a group of volunteer animal lovers from many walks of life including veterinarians; veterinary technicians; staff from shelters, rescue groups and kennels and people who simply loved pets traveled to the islands to set up temporary veterinary clinics they called "Mash Units". Over a two week period they worked with as many animals as possible, spaying and neutering, giving routine care as well as sharing information and materials with local veterinarians and the community. While there, they also offered dog training clinics and all sorts of other pet related activities and services to the people of the Islands.

Compared to how things are done in a veterinary clinic in the States, these Mash Units are rather sparse and simple. A veterinarian's experience of working in a Mash Unit could be likened to working as a medic in a war: you do the best you can with what you have. Although many supplies and equipment are donated for these campaigns, only the basic necessities are available. This can be somewhat uncomfortable for a veterinarian who is used to having all the comforts of his or her home clinic, including a full staff and all the necessary materials.

For most of the Mash Unit volunteers, working in a spay-neuter clinic in a foreign country is a new experience, as well as working with pets who belong to people whose culture they may not fully understand. Sometimes language is an obstacle, especially with medical terms. It is also quite an event for the people living in these islands to have outsiders come in wanting to spay and neuter as many animals as possible, including their pets and any animals wandering about who may seem homeless but who, in truth, actually have homes. And, last but not least, of course it is a major event for the animals!

The campaigns of Animal Balance have been a great success in the Galapagos Islands, nearly eliminating the feral cat and dog problem. They have also helped to form a wonderful bond with the people of the islands. Volunteers and staff continue to visit the islands periodically to keep any newly developing feral populations in check and to continue working with the people there, sharing ideas for pet health and care. Since its success in the Galapagos, Animal Balance has moved on to begin campaigns in the Dominican Republic.

Although the main goal of Animal Balance is to manage the feral populations of dogs and cats in order to protect rare and endangered wild animals, the organization also wants to give dogs and cats the most gentle, loving experience possible in the Mash Units where they are spayed and neutered and given routine care. After getting the campaigns started, Emma asked if I would talk with the "alumni" animals who had gone through the Mash Units so that Animal Balance would understand the experience from their perspective. The idea was to use their feedback and suggestions to make it an even better situation for them.

I agreed to converse with any of the animals who volunteered to talk and set aside a few days to talk with those cats and dogs who had been through the process. We found the descriptions of their experiences to be fascinating and their suggestions for improvement fantastic. Emma has used their suggestions to design and initiate training and guidelines for the human volunteers.

The animals' primary feedback for change centered around both the manner in which the volunteers interacted with the native Islanders and the way the volunteers themselves interacted with each other and the animals. What follows are a series of conversations I had with dogs who volunteered to talk about their experiences on the Galapagos Islands of Isabella, San Cristobal and Santa Cruz, in addition to animals from the first Animal Balance campaigns in the Dominican Republic.

As I settled in to begin conversing with the animals, I had no idea what to expect or even whether any of them would actually volunteer to talk with me. I had asked Emma for some of the details of the campaigns, including dates and the islands on which they were carried out. Sitting at my computer ready to begin typing, I began by taking a few deep, relaxing breaths. I asked if there were any animals connected with the first campaign in the Galapagos Islands from May of 2004 who would be willing to talk about their experiences. I immediately heard a dog address me. He said:

Hello! I am a dog, a red dog. I have moved on.

What do you mean?

I was hit by a car.

Was this after your experience with Animal Balance?

Yes, it was a few years after.

Thank you for volunteering to talk, Red Dog! Is that what you like to be called?

It doesn't matter really. I am reddish in color, in the small to medium size range, with thin short hair with some thin long hairs. I like my look!

What would you like to share about this experience? I think I explained that we humans would like to know what this experience was like for you animals so that we can make changes to make it more pleasant and comfortable for you. What do you think about the idea itself, but especially the experience you had? What would you suggest that might help others have a more pleasant experience?

I felt a lot of stress from the humans in the clinic (Mash Unit). There seemed to be stress about everything. Every detail, including the environment for the incoming humans, was so new for them. I felt all the stress in every human from their entire life up to that time, and stress about being there then. I know it was transformative for them. But I also felt love from them. I was deeply touched by them in a way that I cannot explain. So, on one hand it was an uncomfortable experience, but on the other hand it was so nurturing! Here I was having this surgery that forever altered me physically and then I was so lovingly held by a human. I never had this experience with a human before. After that, I went to my humans and I went to others and started to ask for this love and I was quite often rewarded. My life after that was the richest ever!

I felt great fear going into the clinic. I was not really used to going into a building or shelter of any kind. I only got into the house of my humans when I slipped in against their will, and I soon learned that it was best to stay outside! So, I had some feelings of distress just going into the building itself. I thought I was going to get beat up and chased out, because that had been my experience in the past.

What was it like once you got into the Mash Unit clinic?

Strange! I felt some judgment from some humans. I picked

up thoughts from them that I was dirty and not attractive. I felt some feelings of disgust and I felt they thought they could get a disease from me.

Was this from one person or more?

It was from a few, but mostly from one person who was there hanging around when I came in. She was not the first person I met at the clinic. This first one was kind, but busy. Then I was passed along and was waiting before my surgery. The person who checked on me while I was waiting gave me this judgment. She was a gentle, caring person but seemed insecure and uncomfortable in the Mash Unit setting. Don't worry, I did not take it personally! I just point it out as it can be common from humans coming from very different experiences where they're not used to volunteering in a clinic environment or seeing pets running free in a community, lacking what they might think of as good hygiene. Volunteers could be prepared beforehand to get to know animals of all sizes and shapes as we Island dogs can be rather rough in our appearance. It doesn't mean our humans don't love us because they do. It's just that we live a different lifestyle here and our relationships with humans may be different than the ones the volunteers have with their pets.

Red, how is your lifestyle and the relationship you have with your humans different as opposed to the relationship the volunteers might have with their pets?

From what I have picked up by tuning in with the humans from far away, I see and feel images of their pets sleeping in their beds, and I also see the humans talking with, grooming and cleaning their pets. We live more freely here in the Islands, which we love, and most of us don't sleep with our humans — we usually sleep outside, and we don't mind that at all.

The main thing I wanted to point out is that humans from other lands may think we are mistreated or not very well cared for when they first arrive, particularly if they are really stuck in their opinions about this. They are the ones who miss out because they are closed to getting to know a whole new world of ideas on pet care and the opportunity to have fun sharing. It can cause us a little discomfort too, when we're judged for being a little unkempt, especially when we are waiting our turn for what we do not know.

The human I mentioned earlier was also stressed. It seemed like this one did not have any experience with the clinic and was acting as some sort of an aide who kept us company before we went in for surgery. It seemed like her lack of experience made it so that she feared for the worst. It might help to have a more stable human in this position of waiting with us.

Red Dog, please correct me if I have anything out of alignment here. So you are saying that the person who greeted you initially had an attitude and energy that was helpful to your experience, but that the person who checked on you before your surgery seemed judgmental, thinking that you were dirty and perhaps diseased. In addition, are you saying that this person seemed nervous about your upcoming surgery?

Yes, this is correct. Initially I was not stressed because I did not know what was coming. Well, I was a little stressed being confined and everything, but I was more curious. We don't get all that much excitement here where I live so I was eager to see what was going on. It was when I was there with this particular human who was so worried that I began to fear the worst too. I was confused by her judgment of my lack of grooming as well. That was my worst part of the experience.

But then I was taken by a very loving human who embraced me without concern about either the surgery or about catching a disease from me. This human had an open, loving heart that went beyond judging my physical appearance. I will never forget being swept up with that love. In addition to feeling this profound sense of love, there was also a sense of confidence that all was well. I relaxed right away and soaked up the love. That was the last thing I remembered until that same human looked in on me later as I awoke. I felt like I'd gone to heaven for a little vacation!

I felt rejuvenated in my spirit and ready to face whatever the adventure of life brought my way. Another loving human took me home and I settled back into my life, but it was never the same. I still feel the love of that human. They were all kind and loving, but that one really touched me.

Was this a male human?

Yes it was.

What about your experience in going to the clinic? Did your humans bring you in?

No, some other humans caught me and took me in.

What did your humans think about all this?

71

They seemed to be unsure of it, but they figured, "Why not?" It was like an experiment for them. I was not considered to be such a gift to my family. Basically I was just there, but I was not protected or anything. After this experiment things changed with them and they seemed to look at me with some fascination and curiosity. I took advantage of this attention and went to them for affection and they started to give it. We developed a bond that we never had before. They actually felt sad when I was no longer with them after I got hit by a car. I never thought they would feel anything like that — but we had developed a good relationship. My man really opened up more, but he only did when he was alone with me.

Do you have any other suggestions or thoughts?

Yes, I want to thank these humans. This was a transformative experience and it really brought more peace to our home. Initially I would have fought these alterations (spaying and neutering), but I am now in favor of it. I felt a change right away; many animals were touched and others wanted to be.

Did you notice any changes in your humans?

Yes, they seemed to settle down too. I think I became more of a stable, loving element for them and they settled some as well.

Thank you, Red Dog!

Thank you, Woman!

I paused for only a few moments to focus on my breath and then posed a question out to whoever might want to share about their experience at the Animal Balance clinics.

OK, do we have anyone else from this particular campaign?

Hello, I would like to speak!

Please tell me about yourself and your experience.

I am a dog, a female. I had many puppies and always looked like I was going to have more. I was picked up and taken away by my humans and some new humans who I thought were quite interesting. I felt a little stress at being confined, but I was curious to see and feel them.

You mean to see and feel the new humans?

Yes, they seemed so strange.

In what way?

They seemed to be focused intently on something and some-how I was an important part of that focus. I felt a sense of caring and confidence coming from them.

I relaxed because I felt that it must be OK. Then we arrived at a busy place where I was greeted by more of these humans and quickly taken in. I was unaccustomed to so much attention. They looked me over carefully and talked with me as they went along. At first, I didn't realize they were talking to me, but then it suddenly occurred to me that they were. I was continually feeling the newness of the experience with a subtle yet palpable sense of rising concern, but then I would feel the comfort of their love which felt entirely natural to me so I would relax more deeply again.

The next thing I knew I was in a deep sleep and then I awakened. I felt altered in some way, not just physically, but spiritually too. I cannot explain it, but I felt touched by a loving presence.

Do you mean by the humans there?

Yes and no. It was the humans and something bigger than the humans. I guess because of these humans I see things differently. After the surgery, I felt some soreness and a little tired, but I felt rejuvenated too. I felt like I had a whole new adventure ahead and I began to look to my own humans in a new way. I asked for their love and they began to give it. I feel grateful for the experience — it is like some presence dropped in and shifted our lives. Nothing has been the same since.

What do you mean by that?

Well, I feel different. I feel peaceful and good, more so than ever, and I have more fascination with humans. Before, I did not think about them much except for getting food, but now I have a relationship with them. I look into their eyes and sometimes they look into mine. It is amazing!

Do you have any suggestions for the humans who ran the clinics that would have made the experience more pleasant and comfortable for you?

My experience was fantastic! I do not know what more they could have done for me. I did hear other animals talk of the humans being tired and stressed at some points. My only encouragement would be that the humans be sure to tend to their own needs, perhaps take short breaks even for a few minutes, drink lots of water and eat snacks that they like. Let me turn this over now to another who had this experience.

Thank you!
Is there anyone else who would like to speak?

Me, ME!

OK, please go ahead!

I am a dog, a rat terrier looking dog! I was so excited to be selected!

What do you mean?

I was chosen to go to the place (the Mash Unit)! I met all these humans from another land and I met their animals and other animals too! It was an amazing experience!

Do you have any suggestions for the humans you met?

I was one of the first to go through. I guess my main suggestion would be that they not worry so much about the equipment. I felt their focus on the equipment as a problem and got the sense that they felt really exposed and vulnerable with the equipment they had. I would suggest that they prepare themselves ahead of time by surrendering and accepting that this is all there is. They could take themselves back in time and just relax and remind themselves to do the best they can.

I felt totally safe with them despite their fears because I am a trusting soul and because I was so delighted to be chosen for the mission. But others who are not as confident could really be put off by their lack of confidence. I think the only thing that works is to surrender and let go — this is all you can do. If any of the humans felt that uncomfortable, perhaps it would have been best for them to stay at home. Some will feel that discomfort while others can expand themselves into the experience.

Were all the humans this way or just one or a few?

Most of them seemed to have just arrived and set up the equipment. They were looking at what they had and seemed to be a bit in shock, wondering if they'd made a mistake. Those who did not perform surgery seemed cheery and ready to do whatever — they were fine.

What else?

I would suggest that the people relax as much as possible and that they have a morning meeting like they are a team. It would be helpful if they celebrate the experience of being in another land and of being together. I suggest that they share briefly at the meetings on how things are going, and about the needs of both the group and individuals. For some this might get out of hand, but most humans will cooperate and this exercise can bring greater harmony. Some nice relaxing music could be played in the clinic while they're working too!

Whatever the humans can do to let go and relax and to work harmoniously will help us. If there are conflicts between some of the humans, they can be encouraged to set these aside for the greater cause, to be taken up at another time.

We animals feel conflicts between humans and we feel their unexpressed emotions. Here in the islands we tend to have a lot

of freedom and are not so close to our humans all the time so
we don't have to feel all their fears and irritations. In a confined
area like this, the unexpressed sentiments can be intense and
affect our level of comfort. We ask that you do what you can to
acknowledge your own thoughts and feelings so that you may
find as much peace in being in the Mash Unit as possible and
in this way, it is a wonderful experience for you and for us. It
wasn't bad, but you're asking for our help so I will make this
suggestion here.

In situations where people are taking turns being in charge,
it is important that those who are assisting do so with an open
heart, fully respecting whomever is leading at the time. They
will have their chance. Rest is very important and essential to
good communication in the clinic. We prefer that the staff not
sacrifice their health and energy while there but rather that they
remain in balance by surrendering their control and trust to
another so they can truly rest. The humans who are open about
volunteering and who can take turns leading will benefit greatly.
It is a powerful experience. I saw some of this as they were strug-
gling to get started. They did well and moved through, but some
of them had trouble surrendering and remained in fear because
of the seeming lack of equipment.

Another thing I would like to mention is that we animals
of these island regions often have little experience with being
touched by humans. People from other lands may think this
is sad, but it is not really. I have more experience with being
touched by humans than most, but even I am far less accus-
tomed to being touched than animals from your homeland from
what I can tell.

I would encourage the humans of these Mash Units to avoid touching us excessively. When I was finished with my procedure and waking up, I was being petted and was touched more in those moments than perhaps any other time in my life. I was groggy and somewhat confused. I adapted, but some of my comrades who were unaccustomed to touch from a human were uncomfortable. I would suggest that you touch us very little unless we ask for it and you will know if we want to be touched because we will demand it. We will adjust much better if you just relax and do your thing.

Is there anything else?

No, that is all!

Thank you!

Thank you!

I took a few moments to rest and then asked:

Is there anyone else from this campaign on San Cristobal or from the island of Santa Cruz who went through a Mash Unit there?

Yes, I am a dog. I am unusual for these parts. I was brought in from the mainland just before my experience. I was taken to the Mash Unit just to meet the humans from afar. My human wanted to show me off a little and satisfy her curiosity about who these foreigners were and what was really going on here. Before long, my human was going back and forth in her mind about leaving me at the Mash Unit even though she had intended to breed me. The next thing you know, I was on the table being prepared for the procedure. It was fine for me and made my life simpler, but my human continued to go back and forth about whether she'd made a mistake. She ended up getting another dog with the idea to breed it, but then when the humans came back again the next year, she took that one in too so she could interact with those humans once again. She also brought in some of the neighbors dogs and a cat. It has been interesting watching my human get to know these far-away humans!

Do you have any suggestions for the humans of these units?

In my own case, I saw how the interactions and friendships of the humans from different lands can be so helpful. I would suggest that the humans socialize more, perhaps beginning with a welcoming party for the volunteers to introduce them to the community. That way if my humans meet them right away, there is more chance of interaction throughout the visit.

My people can be a little shy sometimes with strangers. They are very curious and want to get to know others, but they could really use an avenue to do that. Perhaps the clinic leader could go ahead and set up a party and then things will really take off. I think you would be amazed at the developments and how much everything will flow magically. I thank you as this experience has enriched the life of my human and my life too!

Thank you!

Thank you!

Is there anyone else that would like to speak?

I am here!

Please tell me about yourself and your experience.

I am a small to medium size dog of terrier background, but of other things as well! I came to the Mash Unit excited to see what it was. I felt uncomfortable being in a cage, especially with all the activity. It was a bustling enterprise — of what, I did not know — nor did my humans. I was offered up as a research subject. My humans did not appear to be particularly concerned about me, but they really never had been before, at least not that I am aware of. I felt as though I was there to satisfy their curiosity. My humans tried to understand what was happening as best they could and seemed very puzzled at this enterprise. I wondered what was going on and scrambled to get out and be free. Next thing you know, I was being pulled out of the cage and then I started to relax suddenly and quickly. When I awoke I was back in the cage again, but felt like I had been through a trauma of some sort. I did not feel any emotional sense of trauma, but my body was sore and I still felt out of this world.

Are you female?

Yes.
This whole thing was so peculiar to me, but it was not a bad experience at all. I never felt like I was being harmed, I just felt sore when I woke up, but that was not bad. My humans seemed surprised to have me back with them, still alive. It seemed like a miracle to them and they still look at me with a certain curiosity that I cannot explain.

Do you have any suggestions for the people operating the Mash Unit?

I don't know. It wasn't a bad experience really. I like the way my humans look at me as a miracle now. I think this is something positive and I feel like my life is more peaceful overall.

Why do you think your life is more peaceful now?

I think it is the change I feel in my body. I feel like I am of less interest to other dogs and I don't have to struggle so much for everything. I can stay around my home and my needs are met.

Thank you!

Thank you!

I paused for a few moments to rest and take some relaxing breaths. Communing with animals is generally relaxing, but I like to take a moment between conversations. As soon as I was ready, I posed another question to any animals who might be waiting to speak.

Is there anyone else who would like to speak?

Yes, I am a dog. I went through the program and my human was fascinated with the leash. I am still on the leash! It has created a whole new relationship between us and I have been able to teach her many things, my human that is! Sometimes I curse it — the leash, that is — because I really want to run free like I used to, but I still get those opportunities too. I like the way I relate with my human and I will continue to work with her.

How was the experience of going through the Mash Unit for you?

It happened so fast that I really had little time to think about it. It was fine. I found it to be an interesting experience. I would actually have enjoyed staying longer to check it out and experience more. The humans there worked hurriedly unlike anything I had ever seen. I was a little taken aback by their motivation. It felt safe because I felt their compassion, but it kind of swept me off my feet, literally! I am, we all are accustomed to life moving much slower here. That is not to say that moving quickly with direction is bad — it is just different.

Do you have anything else to say?

Only that I felt the confidence of the humans, who had settled into their element and seemed to be at home with what they had and where they were. This made my experience comfortable. I felt like whatever was going on there was going to be OK.

Thank you!

Thank you!

Is there anyone from the island of San Cristobal in the 2006 campaign who would like to speak? (You might wonder how an animal would know the location and year that pertained to their experience. The actual name of the island and the date really mean nothing to them, but when these words are stated, they tune into the Mash Unit, the people involved, etc. and have an immediate connection of having been there or not. They tend to respond instantly to the connection and if they wish to speak, they will.

Excuse me. Let me ask the question again. Is there anyone from the 2006 campaign on the island of San Cristobal that would like to speak of their experience?

YEAH!!!

This time, I felt a number of animals vying for their opportunity to share.

Please decide who will speak and you may begin.

It is me — I am a pushy sort! I am a dog of the esteemed, mixed variety. I like to think of the mystery of my roots as an important part of my charm! I must say that at first, my understanding of what this Mash Unit was all about did not please me.

What do you mean?

Well, I am quite proud of my unknown heritage and I had no idea that the continuation of that heritage could ever stop. It never occurred to me that there was this possibility. I was smuggled into the islands as a tiny creature in the purse of my woman. Once I got a little bigger, she and the rest of the family set me off to the side as their interest went to other things, but this was not really a problem for me because I had so much fun wandering and cavorting with all the neighborhood dogs. Don't get me wrong — the humans and I had some interaction, but it is just that it was not the same after I passed from my cuteness into an adult.

I was living my life as usual when suddenly I was the focus of attention of a group of humans. They were looking at me in-

tently for a few moments as I played with my pals, and the next thing you know we were all gathered and taken into this sort of system (Mash Unit) with humans from another land. Suddenly we were of great interest to humans, but these humans were unlike our humans. They were fast-paced and determined. It was like being whooshed up into a frenzy of activity. I must say that I was startled at first because I was taken so quickly from an easy-going life into a directed activity where the focus was on me! The difference in those people and my own is remarkable, but it is evident that they are of the same human species. And it appears that these humans and my own came together in some common project that suddenly brought attention to our lives. We dogs are unaccustomed to this focus of attention, but it is not all bad, just different.

I immediately started to observe these new humans and I enjoyed myself even in my unusual confinement. I felt the sadness in some of them who believed that I was ragged looking and unkempt — they thought I was obviously abandoned and/or mistreated. These humans seemed to direct powerful emotion towards me and my companions, including some sentiment that I was an unfortunate misfit. I sensed that these humans from another land thought they were here to save me. This surprised me as I enjoy my life and had no idea that anyone had abandoned me or caused me any pain whatsoever. I want to make it perfectly clear here that I honestly do not believe I have been mistreated in any way and that I do not have a problem if I'm dirty or my hair seems unkempt.

I must say that when I was in the Mash Unit it was the most amazing experience for me, one that I will never forget. I was *looked at carefully and talked to. I was petted and I was poked. Then I fell asleep for what seemed like a really long time. When I awoke I had to remember where I was and who I was. I felt the same as I did before going into the Mash Unit for the most part other than some soreness that felt like it could have come from a tussle in the neighborhood. I was greeted by the sounds of these unusual humans and their attention upon me. Once again I was surprised to have this focus.*

Soon I was roaming my neighborhood once more, but feeling different than before as my attention gradually started to wander away from my fellow dogs and to my humans to see what was up with them.

How was this experience for you? Do you have any suggestions for these humans so that they can make it more comfortable for others in the future?

The experience was fascinating. It was one of the highlights of my life and marked a change in me that brought me to more peace and a different relationship with other dogs. I lost my ability to reproduce and my interest in reproducing, but maybe it was time. Otherwise it has been good. My relationship with my humans has become deeper.

What changed the relationship with your humans?

I think it was this event. My interest in humans in general had never been very strong until I met these new humans and was fascinated by how unusual they were. I began to want to spend more time with other humans too, and try to understand and interact with them. I have discovered that humans can pro-

85

vide nearly constant entertainment. I guess that because these humans were so different it made me want to understand them as a species more. I realized that I could continue my investigation with my own humans.

What was it that was so unusual about these humans that captured your attention?

Their focus on us was so intense. Their interest in us was intense, compared to my previous experience with humans where I felt as though I was barely noticed, but yet an important part of the scenery. They also had all this emotion and concern, like they wanted to save us. I felt this as well as judgment about our way of living and some disgust. I don't need to be saved and I like the way I live. But at the same time, in the clinic my interactions were in a manner of the most profound love and respect. I felt I was viewed as being important and that the spotlight was literally on me. I noticed other animals there in the Mash Unit too, and it seemed like they might have experienced something like what I experienced.

The most memorable part of being there was the love and the respect. That has forever touched me and I will never be the same. It has brought me to look to my humans for the love in them. I find it in many ways and I find this experience to be a wonderful and fulfilling endeavor for me.

As far as suggestions, let me first say that I feel grateful to have been part of the experience. It is something that we still talk about here.

What do you mean that you talk about it?

When we animals communicate with one another, it is often a topic of conversation. Those who went through the clinic have something to share with those who did not. We feel proud of it and we all are touched by it in our own unique way.

In some ways it is difficult to evaluate it because of how it has served me, but you are asking, so let me say a few things that could make it less traumatic for the animals who are more sensitive.

It is helpful to keep in mind the difference in the pace of life of my humans as opposed to the humans from other lands. It is an enormous difference that at first had me thinking that they were aliens of another species that in some small way resembled our humans. Even if they consciously slowed themselves down physically, their minds were still going a mile a minute. The minds of these new humans were incredibly active and busy compared to my humans here who often have their focus in the moment, but sometimes drift to memories.

Sometimes these new humans were in other places altogether with their thoughts, but most of the time when they were there with me, they were incredibly attentive. This is another difference between them and our humans here. The attentiveness to us is unusual and it can be intimidating because we are unaccustomed to being the center of attention.

Let me remind you that my overall experience was fantastic and that part of it was because of all these oddities and differences in the humans. I would suggest that you look at us animals with soft eyes and sometimes out of the corner of your eye so you are not so intense. Also keep in mind the pace of life difference and relax. You are a high-powered group that kicked *many things into action here. It was a great stimulus for us all, but if you want it to be more comfortable for us, move a little slower. I assure you that you will still get plenty accomplished. You have captured the curiosity and hearts of many humans and animals here now, so you can settle down a little.*

This is a spiritual aligning for the humans and animals alike, for all of you and all of us. What I mean by this is that it is an opportunity for the realization of oneness between humans with vast differences and between humans and animals. It has even brought us animals together, too!

Having said that, the visiting humans can be reminded that this is our life here. It is very different than how you live in your land and we are doing just fine. What you have come to do is of service to us, but the most powerful thing is the opportunity for oneness. This cause is about oneness, and a consciousness of oneness is the only place where change for the better occurs. I am sure there were numerous moments that seemed magical when humans came together in agreement and understanding, whether it was amongst yourselves or from one of our humans to one of yours. Times like these are what have made this such an overwhelming success.

With this in mind, bonding can be a priority for the team both with one another and with the humans here. This hap-pens with an openness to learn about or know another, not from trying to teach or change another. I encourage the humans from afar to come with as much openness as possible. One of these Mash Unit events can change the life of a human as well as that of an animal; it has changed mine!

The volunteers can be given information about the mission of the Mash Units. This mission can truly serve the highest good for all involved, including those who know about the event and those who are unaware of it because the effects can ripple out to many for a long period of time even after the Mash Unit has closed.

I would also encourage more trust that all will go well, and more use of intuition in deciding how to proceed each day as opposed to deciding in advance. A plan can be made, but be willing to change it if the conditions change. Be flexible and keep in mind the preciousness of a moment in what you humans call time. For instance, if a human of my people comes over to talk with one of you, stop and give your complete attention. Release your plans and be fully present in that magic moment. You may be touched by something you hear that dramatically shifts you in a wonderful way. I would encourage that you take turns interacting with my people so that you can keep your clinic going, but have no fear, it will work out fine and your people will have more energy and enthusiasm when they allow themselves to feel this sense of oneness.

Now, with regard to us animals, we would rather you not focus so intently on us when you look at us or think of us. Many of us prefer not be petted or coddled. We are unaccustomed to this and it can actually increase our stress; it is almost like we are being hunted or something. Please understand that for us, being overly touched might mean running your hand down our back once. If we come to you and rub against you or something like that, you can test it out and give us a little love, but we really would rather be left alone.

We don't even need to be rushed through and out so quickly. It is true that we are unaccustomed to being confined, but we don't mind much when we can be a part of an experience such as this. So take your time and don't worry about running us through your program to avoid stress; instead, move more slowly and peacefully and let us just be there a little longer.

Put your focus and intention on connecting as people. Do not focus on changing the people here, for they do not need to change any more than you need to. Focus on bonding and one-ness, and keep yourselves open to learning about life, and about caring for animals. It may be that your people and mine are at opposite poles and that perhaps something in the middle would truly be best for us animals. Keep your minds open — clear them of the clutter of constant thought.

Bring us in and bring us through the clinic with a soft eye. We are independent creatures having a grand adventure inter-acting with humans and feeling and living our wild roots all at the same time. We love it! We don't mind being "fixed" as you say, but we don't want to entirely change our lives either. Well, some of us do and some of us don't. OK, let me let someone else talk.

Thank you!

Thank you! It has been a great pleasure!

Taking a cue from my new friend, I paused for a moment to catch my breath and relax! Then I called out:

Is there someone else who would like to talk?

It is me! I am so excited to speak! I am a male dog of mys-

terious origin about middle size. I came to the clinic in a hurry just at the end. I might have been the last one to go through. In my normal running around, I kept hearing about all these guys who went there. They seemed different now, but good. My curiosity grew and grew, and I kept putting out thoughts to my human that it would be a good idea to take me to this place (the Mash Unit), but my human was very resistant. I tried everything including sending my human thoughts about my dog friends who went to the Mash Unit, but nothing seemed to change my person. Despite the lack of immediate success, my determination was unwavering and I continued to send messages throughout each day and night. And then finally, I was resting near the entry to the house one morning when my human suddenly grabbed me. I was startled out of my peacefulness, but as the morning unfolded, I began to see images in the mind of my human of me going to this place and I began to feel delight and then fear at what I had put into motion.

When we arrived at the Mash Unit, at the clinic, my human handed me off as though I was a great inconvenience saying, "Here he is, take him." I remember taking a deep breath and thinking, "Oh well, here I go!"

I went through the process and I have to agree with my comrades that it was amazing. Now I am so glad that I persisted and that my human finally responded to my wishes.

What was so great about your experience? What was it like for you and what would you recommend to these humans to make it better for others?

The greatness was in the unique and loving way that

everything was attended to. I am not one for a lot of touch and when these humans first took me in I was petted a lot. I sense that I was petted out of what I believe was the nervousness of this human who was from a far away land. I felt uncomfortable, but I am a stable wise dog and I could handle it. Once I settled in at the Mash Unit, I had the most profound rest with journeys to many lands. I journeyed with the humans there to their lands and met their animal friends. I still remember this distinctly and I continue to visit these new friends of mine on a regular basis.

Let me explain here that once we meet another being of life and join in oneness by opening our hearts, we have access to all that they know and experience. In a sense we are invited to go along on their journey and they are invited to continue in ours. So when I connected with the humans from this far away land, I was able to also connect with their pets and to have an entirely new and interesting experience. I found this to be one of the many benefits of being a part of the Mash Unit.

I did not mind the procedure and I did not have much discomfort. I feel more peaceful in my life now and I have a whole new sense of things that I can barely begin to explain. I feel expanded in my awareness, inspired and delighted. I was quite content before, but now even more so. I am profoundly grateful for your visit to our land, people — thank you!

My only suggestion to these people would be to check in with themselves regularly to see how they are feeling. By this I mean that in a quiet moment or even in a not so quiet moment, you ask yourselves: How do I feel? How am I doing? When you check in like this, you can eliminate any stress or concerns you are carrying but that you may not be aware of.

For instance, the human who was nervously stroking me at the clinic did not realize that she was nervous. If she had checked in with herself often, she would have known when she was feeling nervous and she could have worked with herself to let go of it. It is important for these new humans to keep in mind that they are visiting a far away land and that fears and concerns can come up, so whatever you do for your own comfort, health or peace of mind, you do for us. We animals are like sponges! We pick up on what is going on with you humans, and we do best when you are taking responsibility for your peacefulness and doing what you can to maintain that. As long as you know how you feel, even if it is stress, it helps us because then we are not alone with the awareness of your stress — you are dealing with it.

Thank you!

Thank you!

I took some time for another breather before continuing. OK, is there anyone else who would like to share?

Yes, I am a dog of male gender. I came to the Unit in a roundabout way through people who had heard about the operations there. They wanted to put at least one animal through the system to see how it would turn out. You see, this whole thing is a bit peculiar to my people and to us dogs as well, but I volunteered to go and was taken in.

I went through the camp just fine and enjoyed the presence of humans from another land and all the unusual ideas and things they brought with them. Some of the humans had the smell of their own animals on their clothes. I was able to get to know their animals in this way with my nose. I loved this! I have a very good nose and I like to use it! I have my head down most of the time sniffing and sniffing. It is my heritage!

The one thing that shocked me after going through the Unit was my change in gender; I had no idea this could or would happen. At first I was thinking I'd made a big mistake. When my humans came to take me home, I was given back to them with a leash. My whole life changed going through that camp! My humans took an interest in me like never before. They walk with me on my new leash and they like to show me around the neighborhood. I feel very proud to walk them! They look at me and touch me and play with me. I am enjoying my life!

Do you have any suggestions for the humans of the camp?

No, honestly I do not. Please tell them thank you.

I will, and thank you too!
I paused for a moment.
Is there anyone else from San Cristobal who wishes to speak?
I heard no reply.
OK, is there anyone from the island of Isabela from the 2006 campaigns who would like to speak?

Yes, I am a dog.

Somehow I get the feeling you are from the island of Santa Cruz.

Originally, but I live in Isabela.

MASH UNIT DOGS

Did you go through the clinic in Isabella in '06?

Yes!

OK, please go ahead!

As I was saying, I am a female dog who went through the experience you are asking about. I ran free on a finca (farm) below the volcano and had very little interaction with humans. I was born on Santa Cruz, was brought over as a puppy and set free on the finca, where I had many litters of puppies. Humans paid little attention to me until the day they grabbed me and some other dogs and took us away in a thing that moved. I felt it was my time and that this must be the culmination of this life, but I was not worried or sad like the emotions I have felt from humans on the finca when they believe they are departing. I relaxed more and more as we made our way and then we arrived at a place with humans who seemed rather strange and also somewhat joyous.

I awoke from my surrender to what humans call death and I began to feel more alive than ever. I was fascinated by that place and by the humans and put my attention fully into what was going on there. Despite having little contact with humans in the past, I cooperated as best I could to allow them to look me over, and then I went into a deep rest that was so nurturing. I had not realized how stressful finding food, caring for pups and just living had been for me. I let it all go and it felt so good! I awoke feeling groggy but fine, and before I knew it, I was whisked off back to the finca. My life will never be the same! I have a new life and a new chance because I can take care of me now! No more puppies, and I feel so peaceful and wise! I still keep my distance from humans, but there is something new between us that I cannot explain. I have a greater interest in them and they in me, so we observe each other more. I feel so grateful for this experience!

Do you have any suggestions for these humans?

No, not at all!

Thank you!

Thank you!

I paused for a few moments to rest and then asked:
Is there anyone else from Isabella 2006 that would like to speak?

Yes! It is me!

Please, go ahead!

OK, I was living in the home of my humans. I want to thank these visiting humans for what they brought to my humans and others. My humans were at the clinic nearly every day. They were very inspired by these visiting humans and they made all sorts of changes for me. They learned to walk me on a line or what you would call a leash. I already knew how, but they were having trouble with this. They also made me a new bed from suggestions they got at the clinic — I love my bed! And, I have become a sort of "dog ambassador" of my village. I proudly share information about my experience at the clinic, and others listen with interest. At first my humans did not want me to go through the clinic, but in the end they weakened and put me through. It was difficult for them to have a pet and not partici-pate in the clinic. It was fine with me. I still feel proud and I am an ambassador for the clinic as well.

Do you have any suggestions for these visiting humans?

First, I want to compliment them on the fabulous work they have done with our humans here. We dogs notice many positive changes. I would just say that now they can relax about going to other places and setting up a clinic. If they go in with the idea of celebration and sharing, hearts and minds will continue to open. It would help if they communicate this to the crew. They do not need to convince our humans, they just need to show up, do their thing joyfully and they will attract the people here.

Thank you!

Thank you!

Is there anyone else from Isabella who would like to speak?

I would like to speak.

Please go ahead!

I am a pigeon. I have observed these clinic events with great interest. Sometimes I wish I were a dog or a cat so I could experi-ence it more intimately, but then other times I feel thankful that I am not a dog or a cat!

Do you have something that you would like to share about anything?

Not really, I just wanted to say hello.

Thank you!

Thank you!

OK, let's go to the Dominican Republic for the March and September campaigns of '07.

Yeah!!!! We want to talk!!!

Great! Who would like to go first?

Me! I am a snow white sheepdog, or at least I like to dream that I am! I am really in the tiny body of a small dog, but I am white and I do have a few wild hairs!

I am the delight of my human and go nearly everywhere she goes. I am her baby and I like to make her human children jealous because it is so easy! My woman heard about the clinic and was very curious about it. I kept picking up these images of her taking me there. Despite the images, I was surprised and irritated when she did take me in. Yeah, I know I talked about being a sheep dog. You would think I like to get out in the mud and wrestle, but in reality I am a prissy sort of dog and I am a boy, or at least I used to be! My maleness was about the only assertive part of me so when it was removed, you can imagine that it was quite a shock. Just the thought of being put in the hands of strangers was unusual, but my woman had the greatest respect for and trust in them.

I must admit that I enjoyed the experience. I had never met anyone else who treated me like my woman, but here I was being loved by so many people! It was touching and in the long run, I can now see that it was good. You see, we are not accustomed to this sort of thing here.

Excuse me. What did you mean by "we are not accustomed to this sort of thing here"?

We're not accustomed to being fixed, as you say. Here, it could go either way — the new thing that everyone wants to do or something to feel ashamed of. At first I was not sure how it would be for me, but it really took me to a place of greater understanding of myself. It kind of cleared away many of my illusions about who I am and it helped me to see that yes, although I am a big sheepdog in a little guy's body, I like the comforts of life and I love the attention of my human. I got through the experience and I feel more peaceful and content than I ever felt before. I am delighted and I have become an ambassador here for the clinic, telling other animals about it and helping them convince their humans to take them there when that feels appropriate. I have been involved since the very first clinic.

Do you have any suggestions for the humans at the Mash Unit about how they can make it more comfortable for the animals and for your people?

Yes, I do! I would suggest that they work with the new volunteers coming in on relaxing as much as possible and that they let go of any aspirations or plans to change my people here. It would be better to just come and open themselves to learn about the culture here. If they come to learn, they will learn and share much. Some of the volunteers come in hoping to change the world, and they arrive with the kind of energy and motivation that is somewhat intimidating to our people and to some animals as well. This kind of intention and energy can bring out the fears in the people and it sets up resistance to new information. Our people are so curious that really, all anyone has to do is come with the idea to learn and share. If they are relaxed and not so intense about everything, they will be amazed at how easily the walls come down. True magic can happen in such a setting as this if the humans will surrender to the experience and let it unfold. So, encourage the volunteers to come here open-minded and open-hearted and they will then go home fulfilled and inspired, and our people will also be fulfilled and inspired.

That is all!

Thank you!
Is there anyone else who would like to talk?

Hello, I went through the last clinic event and I want to help others who might want to go through. First, I recommend that the Mash Unit itself be in a more accessible location to our people, and second, that they be taken on as volunteers and made a part of this even more.

Our people are very interested in learning more about your people and they are fascinated to know more about what really goes on in one of these Mash Units and the true motivation of the volunteers. They want to be respectful of privacy, but they also really want to know more. Their visits to the clinic could be a distraction to its mission, but we also know that when our humans interact with yours in sharing information, many wonderful things can occur. In some senses the Mash Unit seems like a dark and mysterious place because so many things about *it seem unusual or different than the experience of our people. By opening the clinic periodically for visits after hours or during breaks between surgeries, curiosity could be satisfied and new bonds of sharing between humans could be established. We also recommend that our people do some volunteer work around the clinic if possible with things that could enhance efficiency or help in spreading the word.*

We see the mystery of the clinic as being what awakens our peoples' interest. The warmth is what encourages them to know more about what you are doing, and the cooperation of those who wish to volunteer is an opportunity for some to feel a part of this.

We see these events as opportunities for the humans more than anything — for the humans who visit and for our humans. The humans from far away can learn as much or more as our humans living here. If they come open to learn, they will and so will our humans! We animals benefit too, but really, it is mostly for the humans. We are grateful! Thank you!

Thank you!

I paused to take some slow deep breaths and felt close to being ready to stop for the day, but I also sensed another animal or two waiting to talk.

Hello, may I speak?

Yes, please go ahead.

OK, I have not been through one of these events, but I want to go through. How can I sign up?

How does your human feel about it?

My human is unaware of it I think.

Do you have any ideas about how your human could be made aware of this?

Yes, I think that some information could be presented at the churches. It could be written information that describes these events and their benefits, or it could be presented in a talk. I saw a human with a rope on it being led by a beautiful dog. I want to have my human on a rope too!

I will tell the woman who coordinates the events (Emma Clifford) about your idea with the churches and in the meantime, you can work with your human to prepare him or her for this opportunity by sending images of dogs and people on ropes together. Hope to see you soon!

Is there anyone else who would like to say anything?

I heard no response.

Great! Well, thank you all from the Galapagos and the Dominican Republic. If you have any other information you would like to share in the future, please do so and I will pass it along to the wonderful woman who initiated this dialogue.

That evening, I emailed Emma my notes from all the animals I had talked with from the various Animal Balance campaigns. She went through them carefully, documented all the suggestions and sent back a summary for me to review. She then asked me to present the summary to the animals to be sure that everything had been acknowledged and also to give them the opportunity to bring up any new suggestions. When I checked with them, they complimented her on picking up on all the important details and gratefully thanked her for her love and concern for their comfort.

Emma asked me to thank the animals for their helpful feedback and suggestions and she began preparations for new campaigns with the added benefit of having their valuable insight.

It has been a few years now since we talked with the Mash Unit Dogs. I always felt their suggestions were so interesting and insightful and wanted to share their story. After writing this chapter, I sent it to Emma for her comments. She responded with the following email:

Hi Maia,

Happy New Year to you too, from me and the 6 dogs and 2 cats that rule my house! With this Blue Moon they are full of beans right now and racing and playing around like nutters. The moon was amazing last night. I was in a yoga class outside as it came up over the ocean — just incredible. I hope that you could and can see it tonight where you are.

I love the chapter — thank you, thank you! It was fun to read what they all said once again. It would be interesting to do a follow-up with them someday to see if things have improved. I hope so. The Dominican dogs certainly do have a good sense of humor; I love that, as they all seem so carefree and happy to me. I think it's perfect Maia; thank you for working with me to improve the clinics for the visiting and resident humans and the animals themselves. More and more people are contacting me for advice about starting similar clinics, so I incorporate the animals' suggestions into the advice I give. So it's getting out there like a spider web now.

Much love to you and have a fun, safe and peaceful New Year!
Emma

P.S. Maybe in 2010 I can talk you into coming to the DR for a campaign...or for a vacation!

I replied with:

Dear Emma,

I was able to experience the blue moon — it was amazing!

Thank you so much for your comments. I agree with you — let's talk with the latest alumni to see how things are going in the Mash Units now. It feels so good to know the suggestions of the animals are being shared far and wide to bring greater peace and comfort to them and to the people involved in the Mash Unit clinics. I love how the animals suggest allowing time for the visiting humans to engage with the Islanders and the profound benefits possible when people unite from foreign lands.

Emma, thank you so much for birthing Animal Balance and for having the dedication to bring together these wonderful volunteers to ensure the continuation of rare and endangered species on the islands while maintaining pet populations and offering free pet health services to the people there, too!

Thank you for the invite, Emma! I would love to join you on one of the campaigns and spend some time in the Dominican Republic too!

Happy New Year to You!
Love,
Maia

CHAPTER SEVEN

Shiloh

I
t was mid afternoon and I was enjoying a few moments with the flowering plants on the patio while drinking a cup of tea and eating chocolate. It looked like another summer storm was brewing. Soon it was time to go back in and complete my final consultations for the day. My next appointment was to talk with a dog named Shiloh. Before beginning my conversation with the dog I re-read this e-mail sent by her human and my response to it.

Maia,

I found you through an Internet search for animal communicators. We recently moved to a new home, but before that, our kitty Beth died. I am concerned that my dog, Shiloh is having serious separation anxiety since our move and our kitty's passing. I need Shiloh to know that I'm not going to leave her. I'm not sure if Shiloh would prefer to be alone because of her advanced age, or if she would be more content with company. Please ask her if it would help to get her a companion animal. She's at the vet today to try and determine her degree of hearing loss and to assess her heart condition. She's been panting excessively the last few weeks and I'd like to know if the problem is stress or age related. I understand that her time with me may be coming to an end and just want to make certain I do everything possible to make her remaining time happy and comfortable.

Thank you, Maia!
Joyce

My response:

Dear Joyce,

I talked with Shiloh this afternoon and have attached her message below. Let me know if you have any additional questions. Thank you!

Maia

Shiloh's Message:

Dearest Woman, I am not having separation anxiety. I am concerned about you! I love you dearly and want you to relax and settle into our new home. I will settle in best when you do. I feel restless and uncomfortable because I do not know if this is temporary or if this is our home for good. I base this on what I am receiving from you, Woman.

You feel restless, unsettled and stressed and it is as though you are not really here with me. You have a million things and plans and projects all going through your mind at once and there is a sense of urgency to get it done fast.

I don't feel at home at all! This is a new place and it would be fine, but we have lost our connection with what brought us here in the first place. You have forgotten our walks, sitting outside and listening to the birds and simply feeling the delight of being together. Sit quietly dear Woman, and take some deep breaths. Walk among the plants. Take in the scents of Nature as you did when you first visited this place. Remember what brought you here and please begin to enjoy your moments here.

Work with yourself to make yourself feel at home, not so much in changing things, fixing things and being busy, thinking you will slow down soon.

Slow down now — this is more important than anything! There is no rush to make changes. You have plenty of time and would enjoy it best taking each project slowly, one at a time, when you truly feel passionate about the project, not when you feel like you must complete it to get it over with. Enjoy each moment, rather than getting the moment over with.

When you relax and settle in, I will too. I am responding to your activity and frenzy of needing to complete projects. You notice my restlessness more because I am like a mirror to you. Before, it was the cat and I both mirroring to you, so it was divided between us and therefore a bit less noticeable. Now since the cat has departed, I am more of a direct mirror to you. The stress you see in me is the stress I feel from you! What you are noticing in me is not age-related. It is stress at being unsettled. At this point, a new animal in the house would only bring more stress. I would prefer to be the only one at least until we are more settled.

I don't need company; I communicate with many friends every day, including the cat. I also feel your companionship and your love. I would like to stay with you longer. Let's focus more on the moment rather than on the future. I will leave at some point and so will you, but we are here now and together. Let's have fun!

Leaving is nothing to fear anyway — really, it is quite marvelous. To think about it brings me feelings of love and a sweetness that is difficult to describe. And you already know that we don't die, we truly live forever.

Do not fret or worry about my health. Put your energy into noticing my good health and into relaxing, rather than in having a negative, worried focus. I love you, Woman, and I feel very happy and fortunate to be with you!

Several days later I got this message from Joyce in my Inbox:

Maia,

Thanks again for your help. The dog's a tattle tale, but she's absolutely right — I've been in somewhat of a manic state since my recent move. I'm working on slowing down and relaxing and Shiloh seems to be much more relaxed and happy already. My sincere thanks and appreciation.

CHAPTER EIGHT

Charles & Calvin

being.

I met Helen through her dog Charles. He was a wise and loving Golden Retriever who somehow reminded me of a warm-hearted Englishman sitting quietly in a cozy den offering kindness and wisdom to those who came to visit, including me! I have actually not met Charles or Helen in person, but Helen has called on me from time to time over the years to talk with Charles about his health and to look in on how to make him most comfortable. Charles had malignant tumors in his nasal cavity that were a great concern for Helen. Despite these challenges, Charles carried on for years until finally it was time to say goodbye. As usual, he gave wise counsel to Helen during his transition of death. Charles's main concern was for Helen. He wanted her to continue on and to find another companion to share her life with. Charles expressed joy in his readiness to make his way to what he called "home". He explained the delight he felt when he thought of being able to fully express his wise and loving spirit without the growing limitations of his beloved physical body. He explained that his body was no longer a clear vessel that allowed his spirit to purely shine forth. He had some wear and scratches that were precious mementos of his journeys and adventures, fond memories of where he had been, what he had learned and most important to him were the playful moments with his traveling companions. He was ready to feel the fullness of his pure spirit and carry with him in his heart forever all those he loved and all he had learned. Charles reminded me to tell Helen that in truth, he was not going anywhere. He would always be at her side — she would not be alone.

Charles gave specific guidance on what he wanted with regard to his transition from his body to pure spirit. He asked to be helped along with euthanasia. His physical body, or what he termed his "vessel", was failing in ways that made it uncomfortable for him to continue. He explained that some of his organs were fine and would keep him going while others were in decline. He could go on, he said, but he would suffer and not be able to carry on in the way he wished to live. So, he asked for Helen's help. He explained when and how he would like to go, and what he wanted her to do with his remains. He requested going into the veterinary clinic he had known for years. He really enjoyed seeing his doctor and the loving staff that kept the clinic warm and inviting for him. For Charles, his visits to the doctor were like social events. The way he described it reminded me of going out for coffee on a daily basis, seeing his old friends. The doctor also admired and respected Charles.

Charles wanted Helen to understand that he could and

would wait for her to feel more ready for his transition. He knew the difficulty we humans have in the transition of death — the fears and confusion that come up for us.

Talking with so many animals over the years who are preparing to make their transition of death and then talking with them after they have transitioned has made it easier for me to understand this. I still feel a great deal of emotion knowing the challenging place this puts us humans in, and I feel the profound connection we have with our dear friends as well as my own memories of being in this very same spot.

Charles made it easier. He felt so solid, so understanding, so loving, so knowing and so much at peace. There is a characteristic feeling I gathered from Charles that I have often felt before from other animals, plants, and even insects. I like to think of this as the energy of the Divine that lives within each one of us. We may have different names for it or a different sense of connection, but in my opinion, and from all I've heard from our dear neighbors — the dogs, cats, horses, etc. we share our lives with — this common feeling is what has them so stable, knowing and loving. Instead of fearing death, they feel steady in it. Instead of us stabilizing and comforting them, they do what they can to stabilize and comfort us. From my interactions with Charles, just thinking of him is stabilizing and comforting on its own. Thank you, Charles!

The instant I said, "Thank you, Charles", I heard him reply with:

"Thank you, Woman!"

It is good to connect with you once again, Charles!

It is a delight to meet you again too!

I wasn't actually planning to talk with you today, Charles.
I was giving a little background information to my readers on
meeting your dear woman, Helen in preparation to tell them
about a conversation with her new dog, Calvin. I could not talk
about Helen without talking about you, Charles! You made such
an impression on my life that I feel you'll always have a place in
my heart.

*Thank you, Woman! The feeling is mutual! I too, enjoyed
communing with you and we'll always be close pals.*

While you're here, Charles, do you have anything you would
like to say?

*Yes, I do! When I felt you thinking of me, I took the oppor-
tunity to come and join you in your mind and in your heart. It is
my desire to speak about the joys of living and the joys of being
human. Of course I am a dog, I'm not a human, but I have had
many moments of studying your kind and loving your kind.*

Charles, it would be an honor to know more about your
views on the joys of living and the joys of being human!

*Great! Let's begin! Woman, will you share the experience
you had where you were awakened in the morning with the passion that we dogs feel in living?*

OK. A number of years ago, I was communicating with
animals of all species on the topic of death so that I could learn
more about their experiences and their understanding of death. I

made myself available to listen whenever and to whoever wished
to speak. Doing this meant that I was awakened at all hours to
listen to whatever any animal might wish to share on the topic
of death. It was kind of like having a twenty-four hour hot line;
I never knew when someone would capture my attention and
ask to share their story or viewpoint. As I listened, I would take
down their messages and ask questions when I felt the need for
greater understanding. This went on for about a month and it
was a fascinating time. In the process, I learned a lot about death
and even more about life.

For instance, I will never forget one morning in particular
when I was awakened by a flurry of activity and excitement. I
felt it within me as well as without. Instead of communing with
just one dog or a few dogs, I was greeted by the presence of one
thousand dogs! I saw them in a soft sense like something out of
the corner of my eye, but they surrounded me fully. I felt their
profound exuberance in being together there, being alive and
sharing a message. They had wagging tails and big grins; their
bodies wiggled and some of them made happy noises to express
their contentment at awakening to a new day and seeing me.

Can you imagine being greeted first thing in the morning by
one thousand dogs? The magnitude of joy I felt was amazing!
Recalling it brings up those wonderful feelings again. I remember asking the dogs, "What's this all about? Why are you here?
What are you trying to tell me?" They quickly responded that
they wanted me to feel their own joy of awakening in the morning to a new life. They explained that, for them, each morning
was not only a new day but a new life, a new opportunity, a
new adventure. They expressed their delight in remembering

and reacquainting themselves with their humans, their environment, and their friends. When I heard this, I immediately had
the thought that I too could celebrate each day remembering my
family, friends, the joys of where I am, where I live, my work and
projects, the opportunities I have, the freedoms I enjoy, etc.

The dogs were delighted that I was catching on to the feeling
of gratitude they have for each moment. As their passion grew,
I felt like it was building inside me too, as though we were one.
It felt so good, yet I also felt some fear. I am a generally happy
person, but this was more joy than I've ever felt. It was intense
and amazing all at the same time. The dogs soon sensed my
discomfort and reminded me to breathe. Ah! The act of breathing
calmed and stabilized me. And then they gradually turned away
to begin their own day with their humans wherever they came
from. The intensity of sentiment quickly and smoothly tapered
off. I was left still lying in my bed feeling all the possibilities of the
day, those dear to me, those who challenge and annoy me, the
projects and the work I have and how I truly am grateful for it all.
Thank you, dogs and thank you Charles, for this reminder!

*You are welcome, Woman! We would love all humans to
have this experience and it is truly available to each of you. All
you have to do is pay $19.95 and click on this link. Just kidding!*

*No, here's what you really do either first thing tomorrow
morning, or right now! I want you to take a few deep, slow
breaths and then think of all the people you really love. Think of
each one and feel the warmth you have in your heart for them.
Allow yourself to really feel the love for a few moments before
moving on to the next person. You can think of your pets too!*

No worries if you forget someone, you can think of them another time. We dogs do not support "worries", not at all! In fact, we would like to help you eliminate that word and that experience from your lives.

OK, let me get back on track here. Revisit your love for your friends, family and pets. Now I want you to ponder all the activities, places, hobbies, things, foods, adventures, etc. that you absolutely love. Ponder some of them and allow yourself to feel the shift in your body. Allow yourself to feel the pure joy you feel when you think of these things.

How are you feeling? This is the way we dogs feel most of the time. We focus on what we love and we feel so grateful for this love we feel that we feel more of it. We encourage you to give yourself the opportunity to take a few moments and think about who you love and what you love and REALLY ALLOW YOURSELF TO FEEL THIS LOVE! Notice that your body begins to feel more alive — it wakes up! You might now have a smile on your face. Your tail could be wagging — whoops! That's right — you don't have a tail! But you can still feel the love. This is the basis for who we are, what we're about and how we like to move in our lives. Imagine traveling through life with this love circulating in you from the ever-present awareness of the love you have in your life. Seriously! Imagine it!

That's my simple wisdom on the joys of living and the joys of being human! I am still working with my woman to get this and I hope that others will like it too. It is so fun! Why do you resist the love and the joy that you so deserve? Just do it! Just allow yourself to wallow in the love and blessings that you already have. Just do it! You'll love it! I promise!

Thank you, Charles!

You are very welcome! Love to you ALL!

All right, let me move along to what I was originally going to share with you, a conversation I had a few days ago with Helen's new dog, Calvin.

Helen was very concerned that Calvin was becoming aggressive towards people. He hadn't always been this way; in fact, he used to be rather quiet and reserved. Sometimes he was scared when people approached him without warning, but for the most part he was easy going. But recently Calvin had demonstrated behavior that worried Helen very much; he seemed to have a more aggressive posture, he growled and she feared that he might bite someone. Having lost her dear Charles only a few years before, the last thing she wanted was to have anyone harmed or to have to put Calvin to sleep. She feared the worst.

Helen scheduled a time for us to talk at 4 p.m. in the afternoon. Just before I called her, I took a few moments to breathe and clear my head from my last appointment. I was eager to talk with Calvin to gain more understanding of his behavior and any solutions he might suggest to bring harmony and joy back into their lives.

I took a few moments to converse with Calvin to find out what was going on before calling Helen.

Hello Calvin!

Hello Woman!

Calvin, do you understand why we are talking today?

Of course! I know the concerns of my woman. I know her confusion too. I know she's worried that I will hurt someone and that she might have to let me go, or what she thinks of as taking my life. She feels very stuck and very sad about this — I know!

Calvin, why are you becoming increasingly more aggressive? If you know the concerns of your woman, why do you carry on with this behavior? Why not just stop? I'm asking you this because people ask me these questions all the time. For instance, "If my dog loves me and he knows this behavior makes me feel stressed, why does he keep doing it?!"

Let me explain. I am fully dedicated to my woman. I like to think of myself as a beacon of love and wisdom here to support her in knowing her most inspired and loved life. I am dedicated to this at all costs, even if it means that I depart from what you humans think of as this world. My ultimate goal is for her to experience great peace and joy each day, in each moment. But, in order for her to experience this, she must allow a new under-standing to come into place. As long as she continues as she is, peace and joy are very difficult to achieve. Yes, I am causing ad-ditional stress in her life, but it is for the purpose of encouraging a big shift that will bring her great joy and peace. She can either handle this challenge as an additional stress and go on as usual, or it could be serious enough this time, with my life on the line, for her to be inspired to change her life.

Calvin, what is it that you so want your woman to change?

As long as she continues to focus on the down side of humanity and to keep it alive in her mind, her heart will be heavy. If she were to open herself to know the simple beauty within each human, she would have a whole new vision of life.

When my woman changes her beliefs about humans, so will I!

What do you mean by this, Calvin?

Ask my woman!

At this point I decided to go ahead and call Helen. Once I had her on the phone, I began to explain my conversation with her dog and ask her some questions to help bring clarity to their situation.

Helen, Calvin indicates that he is merely following your lead in this. He says that his aggression is based on something you are thinking or doing.

Helen immediately responded, "Well, I do talk with him every day about the dangers of humans. I tell him to be careful. He is a beautiful dog and someone might want to steal him. I also tell him that people abuse animals all the time and that someone could hurt him. I talk with him like this every day."

"Thank you Helen," I said, "let me talk with Calvin again." But before I could say anything to Calvin, he responded to the words of his woman.

That's what I'm talking about! As long as she tells me this story I am going to act it out. She is giving me the script of her own fears and I am demonstrating her aggression and fear and hatred in regard to her fellow humans. As I said earlier, when

120

she truly changes her beliefs, so will I. I actually do not agree with her, but as I said before, I am dedicated to her being able to live her most fulfilled, inspired life. It is impossible for her to do this while maintaining this kind of negative belief about her own species and ultimately disliking herself, too. I stand firmly in this as long as she does.

What do you suggest, Calvin?

I request that my woman begin an assignment. I request that each day when she goes out into the world, she seeks out examples of love and kindness. I request that she allows these incidences to fill her mind — that she thinks about these incidences, imagines them again and then allows them to fill her heart with love and peace. I request that she allows these stories to warm her heart and then I request that she tell me these stories when we return to our home.

Share them from your heart so that I may experience the simple beauty of the human heart. I want to feel this through you, Woman! I want to know this feeling through you. If you do this on a daily basis you will open yourself to experience the love that you so desire and that you so deserve from your fellow human kind. And, if you do this, I too will begin to feel this love through you and I will be able to settle into my true peaceful, loving self and enjoy humans as well. Let's celebrate the beauty that is so profound in the spirit and heart of every human being. Let's celebrate it and enjoy it so that it has the opportunity to enjoy its full and beautiful expression here on Earth.

Woman, you tend to focus on the "bad" things humans do. You add another item to the list of why you hate your fellow humans each moment as you focus on finding more reasons to dislike your own species and yourself. I request that you do the opposite. That does not mean sweeping your frustrations under the rug. Acknowledge them, but that does not mean grounding them into your mind and heart over and over again. Acknowledge them and then once again, seek out those bits of magic of humanity that are so prevalent and so profound. We animals see them all the time! That's why we look at you with such admiration. That's why we love you so much!

Calvin, I understand what you're saying here, but I know some humans are going to wonder why you are so insistent on continuing to be aggressive when you know it would be so much easier for your human if you just quit and you were your sweet, loving self and you let her think negatively about her species and herself if that's what she wants.

Like I said before, I love my woman! I want her to have her most fulfilling and inspired life. I am dedicated to act out for her what she refuses to look at as the basis of her unhappy life, which is a continued focus on all the "bad" things her kind does. If she were to look at me with that kind of focus, she would probably not like me either. I have gas and sometimes my breath smells bad. I like to chew on her stuff. And, I now have this aggressive behavior that stresses and concerns her, yet she continues to adore me no matter what. I am asking her to find the fun and the compassion and the love in her own kind so that she will live with those joys each day and ultimately so that she will fall in love with her own dear self. I love her so much! I will do anything to help her find this love, even if she decides not to open herself up to the joy of being human.

Thank you Calvin, that makes good sense. What can she do in the meantime while she is making these changes? Will you stop your aggressive behavior now?

I will not stop until she does. She cannot fully trust me until she fully trusts herself. I suggest she put a muzzle on me when we go out, but it is very important that she not use the muzzle as the cure. The cure is what I requested — it is her assignment to find the sweetness of humanity every day, even if it seems like a tiny thing.

Find it and feel it in your heart, Woman, and then share it with me. I want to hear about it in your daily storytelling and I want to feel it through your feeling it.

When you say "find the sweetness" please give me some examples of what you mean.

It could be something on the television or radio, some good deed. It could be some kindness given to another in the market or on the highway. It is there! It is everywhere to be seen and felt because humans are basically good and kind-hearted beings. It is confusion and lack of self love that bring about unkind acts; the more that humans focus on violence, the more unkind and horrific acts will occur. Your human information-sharing is aligned toward sharing violent events and acts. But there are even more profound acts of kindness each day, yet they often fail to be acknowledged. The vibrant health of your species depends on remembering the profound love that exists within each human and giving this love the kind of attention it deserves. We suggest that you celebrate it all the time — each day — and to welcome this truth into your reality. It resides in the hearts of all. Why not allow it to be felt and known on a wider scale? If you imagine a dog such as myself and others of my kind, the most common image is of love. We exude it and we celebrate it because that is what we are! We are love — and so are you!

The next day I received this email from Helen:

Hello Maia,

Thank you so much! I really appreciate your help with Calvin. I'm going to get Calvin a muzzle for when we go out and work on changing my outlook on things.

Thanks Maia!
Helen

A few weeks later Calvin captured my attention by spontanously joining me in my mind; I suddenly could think of nothing else but Calvin. He requested that I check in with his woman. So I sent her the following email:

Hi Helen,

Calvin dropped in this morning to ask me to check on you. He wanted me to ask you how you are doing with your assignment from our last conversation, and to see if you have any questions about it, etc.

How's he doing? He's not really telling me anything other than to check on you.

Love to you both!

Maia

Later that day I received a reply to my message.

Dear Maia,

I'm working on it!
Thank you for the reminder, Maia!

After reading Helen's email, I decided to check with Calvin to see if he had anything else to say.

Calvin, how are things going?

Not a lot of change so far. Humans tend to resist change, especially when it means they might have more contentment. It seems too easy — they actually seem to have an aversion to simplicity, peace and joy. But, I am very patient! I believe that one day my woman will choose this for herself! It is really up to her. I love her no matter what!

Thank you, Calvin!

Thank you, Woman!

CHAPTER NINE

Orson

O rson is my wise and lovable neighbor. He's a Golden Retriever who always greets me enthusiastically with a wagging tail and a huge grin. He has a way of lifting his lips up so you can be sure to capture his smile — he really wants you to know he's smiling! That infectious smile goes right to my heart and causes me to smile too. Orson and his people are my dear friends. I always enjoy meeting them out in the neighborhood and sometimes I'll see the three of them out walking on the red rock trails. Orson leads his people on walks to the grocery store and past the coffee shop. On a few occasions I happened to be inside the coffee shop and saw Orson walk nonchalantly past the entrance as if he were out walking on his own, but sure enough just as I was about to go check on him I saw one of his humans coming along behind him on the sidewalk. Orson loves to get out and greet as many people as he possibly can. It seems as though he has an abundance of love emanating from him that he absolutely must share.

Orson is the dog you see with me on the cover of this book. He eagerly volunteered to join me in the photos and was so much fun to be with. When I was preparing for the photo shoots I was gathering supplies to take along while he was at his home across the street. Even though I had not been over to his house he always knew we were going and he waited excitedly inside my neighbor's door in anticipation. When he heard me out in the street putting things in the car he would start to bark and carry on. I would go get him and we'd head out to the trail with Pam Taylor, our photographer.

I talk with Orson briefly whenever we meet, but for about a year, I have wanted to take some time to really listen to and talk with him at length. I tend to keep busy with conversations with my clients' pets, writing books and all the other things of life so the desire to talk with Orson has stayed with me, but up until now, has not been satisfied. When I decided to put together a collection of dialogs with dogs I knew I wanted to include Orson and give him the opportunity to speak, especially since he so graciously volunteered to have his photo taken for the cover of my first book, and we ended up choosing a photo of the two of us together for this book as well.

As this book was coming together, I still hadn't talked with Orson. Finally under the beautiful blue moon of the New Year, I awoke very early and knew that we could at last have our conversation.

This conversation with Orson is a little different because I was not asked to talk with him by his people. I just wanted to simply give him the opportunity to speak on whatever topics he wished and I planned on asking him questions as we went along to be sure he was understood.

As I prepared to listen to Orson, I paused as I normally do to appreciate a few conscious breaths, then I began to feel his warm, lovable personality coming through. I greeted him: Hello Orson!

Hello Woman! At last I get to speak!

Yes, at last you do, Orson! I've wanted to get to know you more for a long time. I love your warm greetings and your enthusiasm for the humans you meet each day. I'm all yours, Orson! Please share whatever you would like to share, and I promise I will make your message available to other humans.

Yea! OK, let's pause for a moment to breathe.

OK.

I want to talk about running while I have these moments. I love to run and many dogs do! We run around celebrating how wonderful it feels to be in our bodies, to be free and to feel good. I don't run so much anymore. It's only when I am running up to greet someone, or when my enthusiasm is more than I can hold and it comes out of my pores and into the environment. But I run and I play in my dreams. My spirit is lively and bold, sweet and kind. I am warm and loving like you would think of how a Teddy Bear is. I just want to say that even when you don't see us dogs running anymore — even when we have really slowed down — we run, we play and we celebrate life. When we're slowing down in our life it's like we're wearing a Halloween cos-tume that limits our movement. We are just as alive and playful as ever, but we are limited in our expression of our joy or exu-

berance by the costume. We are not our bodies, our costumes. They serve us in being our suit of expression so to speak for the adventure of life, but they become worn and tattered over time. We dogs just want you humans to remember that what you see on the outside is not really who we are — it's just our costume this time. When it looks tattered and worn, when it moves slowly and when maybe it looks sad to you, it's not necessarily the truth. We're in there, in the costume as full of life and love as ever; it's just that we have difficulty showing you through the old costume. It doesn't move like it used to and it just doesn't look like it used to.

The main thing I want to say on behalf of the dog is that we never lose our enthusiasm or our sparkle for you or for life. We are bursting with love and delight and so eager to share it, but you must look beyond our surface, you must commune with us in a deeper manner. Close your eyes; take them off our bodies and really listen to who we are and what we have to say. You truly can hold our preciousness, our sweetness and our love forever in your hearts and in your experience. We never really change; it is only our bodies that change. Remember that we are not our bodies — we are purely of spirit, just like you! You are not your bodies either! We know this and that is why we look deeper into you to know who you really are. We love what we find there and we encourage you to look deep within and get to know your true spirit too.

Orson, how do you suggest we get to know our own true spirit?

Remember that you are not your body, your job, your

130

clothes, your car, your sport, your toys, your tools, your home
or your partner. You are you, pure and simple. If you think of
yourself without all that, if you imagine you are like us without
any clothes attached, no property, no nothing, you will see what
I mean. This is who you really are, but I encourage you to go
deeper. Without all your outer trappings you might feel naked
and empty, alone and desolate. It's not that way and I'm not
suggesting you give all that up. The trappings are there for you
to play with and enjoy. All I'm saying is that they aren't you!
You are your own pure self without any trappings. When you
look at yourself this way just as you are, how does it feel? To us,
it feels so light and so free. We don't worry about our next meal
or anything. We know that we will be provided for one way or
another. I'm not suggesting that you stop working or give up all
the things you have; all I'm suggesting is that you take a different
perspective. You might find that you like yourself more than you
realized or that you don't, and you can grow to care more deeply
for yourself with greater awareness of who you really are. We
dogs have a very light way of being because we live in love —
love for ourselves, love for our fellows of other species, including
humans, and love for the opportunity to be here dancing!

Orson, how will we know when we have found our own
true spirit? What is that like and why do you suggest this?

The way to access your own true spirit is to take moments
each day for yourself. Everyone (you humans anyway) seems to
busy themselves with tasks that fill your days and your tomorrows. There seems to be little time to just be. We dogs suggest
you keep in mind that your tasks will never end. It is important

to find moments to pause and simply be as this is what life is truly all about. We dogs know how to do life well!

What I'm saying here is this: If you find a way to remind yourself to pause, if even for a few moments and allow yourself to breathe and relax, you will begin to experience your life in a new way. You may begin to really appreciate these moments and find ways to enjoy more of them. The simple act of pausing to focus on your breath can give you a wonderful reminder of what's really important, and that is the fact that you are alive. This is a wonderful blessing and something that really brings new perspective and insight into all the things you are involved in.

The simple act of focusing on the breath brings you back home to what is true, to your roots as a Divine being of life and to the understanding that all beings are connected in oneness in the moment of a breath.

It is not necessary to sit and meditate for long periods on the breath, although some will enjoy doing this. A few moments of focus periodically throughout a day can make an amazing impact on your life by bringing you a greater sense of stability, peace and fulfillment. These few moments of focus are a way of communicating with yourself and giving to yourself because the breath is literally a gift of life to birth the physical essence of your spirit into being. Each time you take a conscious breath, you celebrate the birth of your spirit in your own unique physical form and you celebrate life. This is why I like to pause in my day to enjoy a few breaths and celebrate my presence here on Earth.

When we focus in this way, we make a profound statement that ripples out to every cell of the physical self, letting it know that it is important and appreciated. We give comfort to the *spirit self by saying hello with the breath. Do we dogs do this? Of course! That is why we're so happy all the time! We love this practice and we love our lives.*

We recommend it very strongly because we want our human species to come alive with passion for life. We want you to remember that you are Divine beings just like us, and that you have an abundance of energy in the form of love available to you in each moment if you will only pause to receive and enjoy it. We fill ourselves automatically and continually with this energy. The love we feel and receive in the breath fills us and overflows into our environment to our humans and out to greet all our fellow beings of life. This is why we're so jolly, and why humans like to have us around. We are tapped in and taking advantage of the Divine love that is available, so we are abundant and overflowing with love.

You humans actually feed off our flow. We don't mind this at all, but we want you to access your own flow of energy so that you can feel it coming in from your own source and so you can truly fill yourselves to the brim and let it pour out to all your fellow beings of life in gratitude like we do.

When you tap into your own energetic flow, you are full all the time. Then other humans may want to be around you more often to unknowingly tap into your energy, just like humans hang around dogs and other animals to tap into theirs. You can encourage and inspire fellow humans to benefit from their own personal flow of energy, too.

We, your fellow beings of life, the animals, plants, even and especially the insects and the Earth itself, all are highly attuned to our Divine beginnings and to our energetic alignment. There is

access to and awareness of this, except humans. You have full access to Divine love and light, but you lack awareness of its presence and availability; hence, you often live cut off from your natural energy source and you feel deprived and depleted. It can have you in a state of irritation even when you want to be kind and caring. You come from a place of emptiness because of your lack of awareness and sometimes your lack of desire to allow the flow to come into you in all moments.

Because of the lack of awareness and appreciation of the abundant energy source available to all humans, you live in a state of desperation and sometimes even despair. You compete with one another for limited energy sources and you have a sense of limitation in regard to those resources. So you take from your friends, your parents, your children, your natural environment and your dogs.

There is a feeling of emptiness and irritation because something is missing — something so essential that fits perfectly into your Divine base like a key that is designed perfectly for a particular lock.

So you're going around trying to live life without being hooked into your base. You have all the equipment and all this energy flowing through it to your base, but you shut the little door that would allow it to be flowing into you naturally in all moments.

You've closed off the entry by your lack of awareness of the importance of this energy to you. It's not a serious problem. All you have to do is open the door by reminding yourself of who you really are, a Divine being of love and light, and that you love yourself enough to allow yourself to receive all the energy that is naturally and abundantly available to you.

Remind yourself of who you are each moment of each day!

Being supposedly cut off from your Divine source of love and light is both an individual situation as well as a species-related situation. What I mean by this is that individually it is now necessary for each one of you to decide to open the floodgates and to continue to strive to open them more and more. It is a species situation because it is something that was dictated to many members of your species long ago by a small group seeking to control the majority. The small controlling faction planted and nurtured the idea that you were not deserving of love, kindness and respect. It was passed along that it was harmful to love the self and inappropriate to do so.

But love of self is the gift of the Divine and love is the basis of all life! When love was taken away from the self, the connection from the Divine to the self was obviously ignored and many humans began to feel disconnected and they passed that confusion on to their children.

We are all beings of the Divine. The Divine is all about love — that's what we're literally made of. If we believe it is no longer appropriate for us to love ourselves, then we can no longer have a connection with the Divine and therefore we might conclude that we ourselves are not Divine.

There are some mistaken "truths" here that must be evaluated on a personal basis as to what feels correct for each individual. But I am here to tell you that YOU ARE DIVINE! And that means that loving yourself is good and even necessary. In fact, it is required that you love yourself in order to reclaim your heritage and to reclaim the energy of love and light that is yours each moment to fill you full of love, which can overflow out into your environment to uplift others who are finding their way.

Part of the decision to open up the natural flow again is to make a commitment to self love and to the understanding that this journey never ends. If you think you love yourself enough, you are incorrect. You are simply holding back from going deeper. Commit to self love and to going deeper and to loving more all the time. You have a lot of catching up to do! Don't stop; keep exploring other ways to love you because when you do, you open those floodgates even more, you feel the love flowing through you and you feel inspired and fulfilled all at the same time.

As you open up more and more, we don't feel you feeding off our energy. Instead, we feel your fullness and this makes us very happy. When one human opens him- or herself to the ongoing journey of consciously breathing in the Divine energy of love, other humans are unknowingly inspired to awaken their own appreciation for the breath and the understanding that this is the doorway to their own energetic source of love and light. This is how one human inspires another and another and another. The more humans who appreciate their own abundant flow of Divine energy of love and light, the more peace there is because people are full and satisfied. They come from a place of peace and fullness in their decision-making and this means they come from a place of kindness and compassion toward themselves and toward all beings of life, maybe even insects!

This is why we dogs and other animals push humans on this so much! We want you to find your peaceful, loving base so that we (all beings of life) can all stand joyfully in love and light. We love you; you are our brothers and sisters! We want you to feel the profound joy that we feel simply in appreciating a breath of

Divine love and light. As more humans remember this, more love and light will be appreciated and experienced on our Mother Earth. The energy of love and light bounces back and forth from those living in the natural flow out to all beings. The more awareness there is, the more love there is bouncing back and forth between beings of life. We're already there engaging with love; we've always been there engaging with love because we never cut ourselves off from our Divine source of love and light. It is our hope for humanity that you remember your Divine roots and join us in the true dance of life.

Orson, wow, I feel really touched by what you're saying and I feel inspired to open myself even more to this natural flow of energy available to me. Will you give us some suggestions for how we can specifically do this?

The bottom line is to always choose love; choose love! Make this a new habit. It is clearly evident whether you are choosing love or self judgment by how you are with yourself. How you speak to yourself, think about yourself, feed yourself and care for yourself is based on whether you love yourself. This is a choice! Whatever has you feeling alive and inspired is a choice of love for yourself. Whatever has you feeling stagnant and irritated is a choice that goes against nurturing and loving you. Begin to notice what makes you smile, what has you feeling uplifted, rejuvenated and refreshed in the long run. When you pause to focus on your breath, you naturally tune into how you are feeling, you naturally nurture yourself and you consciously open yourself, for at least a few minutes, to receive your Divine energy of love and light. The goal is to open yourself to receive in all moments, but it is challenging for you humans to give love to yourselves when you are feeling irritated with yourself. In order to receive the love and light of the Divine you must truly agree to love yourself; you must actually love yourself.

Be with yourself like you would be with your beloved child or your beloved dog. You want them to receive all the love available, so do this for yourself. It happens each moment of each day — you choose love in each moment and with each breath. That is all you have to do; keep choosing love! In the process, many old mistaken ideas will come forth to fight your new choice. It will be an opportunity to greet them, see how they no longer feel true and to release them.

This is really simple, just let love be your guide. We love you and our presence is a constant reminder to love yourselves. Do you think we love ourselves? Of course we do!

Orson, I've always looked to dogs and wondered who you really are. It seems like you're always greeting a new day and a new person with an amazing amount of enthusiasm. You seem to be so consistent in this way. Who are you really and why are you like this?

We are Divine beings of love and light and we know it! We are so full and so bursting with energy directly from our source that we cannot contain our expression of love and enthusiasm. We cannot contain it, nor do we want to. We want to share it with all of you and inspire you to go within, love yourself and fill up on the love and light available to you!

OK, here's a question I get often from people curious about

my conversations with dogs. Why, when you meet another dog do you sniff their butt?

That's a good one! That's kind of like the question: "When a tree falls in the forest and no one (human) is around, is there a sound?" If no humans are watching, do we still sniff another dog's butt? Yes we do! Heads and tails — it's fun! We sniff noses and we sniff butts. Sometimes we sniff butts first. Sometimes we get distracted and sniff the head or the butt and then wander off without sniffing the other end. This is merely a form of greeting for our species, kind of like how you humans shake hands. We are not shy about sniffing butts; we're really not shy about much of anything as a species.

Thanks Orson! Why do dogs often sit and look deeply into our eyes?

It is because we are attempting to connect with you deeply. We are trying to get your attention and we want to take you deeply inside yourself to know how wonderful you humans really are. We want you to know the profound opportunities for creation you have at your Divine core. When you notice us looking into you like this, we encourage you to pause for a few moments from your activity, to breathe and join us in oneness. You will feel and come to know many things of life by taking these moments to join in oneness. Will you join us? All of you?!

Orson, what do you mean by "All of you?!"?

I mean all of you, anyone reading this book, all humans.

Do you like living with humans? Why would you choose this

when we're feeding off your flow of Divine energy/love?

In most instances, we enjoy living with you and we find you to be immensely entertaining. We choose to be with you and, as I mentioned previously, it aligns with our overall purpose as dogs to bring you home to an understanding of who you really are and why you are here in this experience of life. Occasionally, we might regret our choice of a particular human or a particular assignment, but most of the time we are delighted with our work and we feel fulfilled and satisfied in living in alignment with our purpose.

We choose to live with you humans even though you often feed off our energy of love and light because it is our purpose and because part of helping you find your way is sharing this energy so you'll recognize it when you find your own connection with your Divine source.

Thanks! Orson, people sometimes believe that dogs are not so intelligent because you seem to give your lives up for your human companions — you're often agreeable to whatever we seem to want and sometimes you're really silly and you seem to be so dependent upon our care. Do you have anything to say about this to help us humans have a greater understanding of dogs and perhaps of ourselves?

What you say is true. Many humans think we are not very intelligent but once in awhile they'll run across a dog they believe to be particularly intelligent. What's interesting is that usually the animal the human believes is so intelligent is somewhat more similar to a human in its way of interacting than other dogs. What I'm saying here is that when an animal acts like a human in any way, it is assumed that they are intelligent for their species. In reality though, sometimes they are not as intelligent as some of the animals who seem to lack intelligence from the human perspective. Let me further explain. Whatever a human considers or explores is done from their particular understanding as an individual, but also from their understanding as a human. When a human engages with an animal and if the animal engages back in a "human sort of way", the human feels connected and he or she naturally feels good. The person assumes instantly that this particular animal is highly intelligent for an animal. Let me point out the basic assumption that the interest and ability to effectively engage with others is an indicator of intelligence. In some senses this is true because effective communication can certainly come from intelligence. But what if an individual simply would rather not engage with a human? Or what if they want to engage with the human but not in a way that a human would normally think to engage? For instance, what if they want to engage with a human in a deeply spiritual way? What if they want to stretch the abilities of the human to join them in another and perhaps an even more sophisticated manner of engaging? Does that mean they lack intelligence? Usually if an animal doesn't engage with a human in a "human" way by making eye contact and giving attention back to the human, the assumption is automatically made that they have little intelligence. Many humans don't even believe that animals have a soul or spirit.

I am here to tell you the truth, that beings of life have their own unique manner of expressing and engaging with one another. The animals you humans commonly think of as being dumb are really quite intelligent and they are engaging with you in all *sorts of ways that are truly brilliant without your awareness that they are engaging at all.*

I would encourage humans to keep in mind that we are different than you. This does not mean we are dumb. We love you dearly and don't take your lack of awareness personally. We encourage you to open yourself to the truth that there is an amazing amount of intelligence all around you.

We dogs are an engaging lot and this is why we are considered to be your best friend. The way we engage is often with silliness and play; but we are actually the wisest ones. Those more serious and humanlike are often less aware of themselves.

If you take a few moments to ponder your human population, the most stable and loving and the truly wise beings are also often the most playful and silly. Take, for example, the Dalai Lama. He is one of the most light-hearted, playful and silly beings on Earth and he is also perhaps the most enlightened being we know here at this time. He is so full of love and light, like we are! He is playful and kind, laughs all the time, yet he is absolutely brilliant and in touch with all his capacities as a Divine human being who is constantly overflowing with love and light that pours out to so many others who have yet to find their own connection to their source. He greets everyone and every day with joyous gratitude and love because he is filled with it and overflowing.

This is how we feel too, and this is our wisdom!

That's interesting Orson, and reminds me of a wonderful dog I knew years ago. Lacy was always so happy. She had this huge grin on her face and wiggled her body excitedly whenever she greeted someone. She always seemed to be overflowing with joy. It is interesting that people really thought she was dumb. I remember talking with her on a few occasions and learning about all these amazing truths and adventures she'd had. She'd even traveled with Buddha at one point in one of her past experiences. I got that sense with her about what you're talking about when we humans tended to think she wasn't very smart because she was ridiculously happy all the time. Her needs seemed to be so few and so simple. She radiated so much love out to her environment and, as I found out, so much wisdom too!

Yes! This is true and a good example of what I'm talking about. I want to answer another part of your question. You mentioned that we dogs tend to give up our lives for our humans as if we don't have an agenda or things we want to do for ourselves. It is true that we have come to serve. As the closest beings to the human species, it is our purpose to be close to you and help you awaken to the awareness of who you really are. This is our purpose, so we're right where we're supposed to be. We're not giving up anything; in fact, our goals are rather selfish in a way because when humans awake to the love and light energy available to them, our entire planet and all beings of life will be uplifted. As much as we love you, the human species is a drag on all the other species, including the Earth. We want you to wake up and love yourselves so that you will love each other. Then and only then will you truly be able to love your dog, your cat, your horse, the rose bush, your hamster or your child because only then will you be allowing yourself to be filled with the love and light of your Divine roots. Only then will you be overflowing with love and able to share it with other beings of life. You must love yourself first!

CHAPTER TEN

Little Orphan Annie

From the moment Elizabeth saw the photos of Little Orphan Annie and read her story in the paper, she wanted to adopt her. Annie was a dog who had been removed from an abusive situation. She was living in a shelter receiving veterinary care with the hope and plan that she would eventually go to a new home. I got a call from Elizabeth one day with the exciting news that she had at last adopted Little Orphan Annie. While getting to know her new dog, she noticed Annie had some skin problems, so she contacted me to talk with her to gain some insight into these health challenges, and to ask what would make her most comfortable and content in her new home.

By then, I had been hearing about this dog for weeks and was happy for Elizabeth that her dream had finally come true. I felt quite excited about meeting her at last so I worked with myself to settle my feelings of anticipation by taking a few moments to breathe and calm myself. As soon as I felt ready I greeted her.

145

Hello, Little Orphan Annie!

Hello, Woman!

How are you settling in Annie? Do you like your new home?

I love my new home and my new woman! I feel so delighted to be here with her sharing our lives together! I felt her interest in me and I was so excited to get to meet her and to begin our new life!

L.O. Annie, your new woman has some concerns about your health and contentment. Do you have information to share with her to help alleviate any confusion that she has and to help her care for you in the best way possible for your unique needs?

I do! I have specific instructions that I will list. Before I do though, let me mention that I am considered to be a victim, a rescued dog with a rough past. I really don't want that label! People look at me and give me a sad look; my woman does sometimes, too!

I am a champion! I want to be thought of that way. As long as I am thought of as a victim, I will continue to have one problem after another. I am finished with this! I have not been rescued, I have been adopted! There is nothing to rescue me from! This is number one on my list of important changes for my woman and it is also a message to any other humans who care to listen.

Little Orphan Annie, would you please explain what you mean by that last statement?

Yes. What I said was that there is nothing to rescue me or us from. The incredible number of animals in shelters today and those who are being abused come from thoughts of needing to rescue. As long as humans are in a mode of thinking, talking about and focusing on the injustices done to animals, this becomes the reality. More and more injustice is created because more and more people have chosen this to be the reality: that life is all about animals being abused and abandoned. And, with more and more people thinking this way, there will be more and more animals in this situation to satisfy the reality of the humans. Am I making sense here?

Yes, I understand what you are saying, but how do we get from where we are to where we want to be? Basically, how can we make it so there are no animals abused, no animals abandoned, and ultimately that there are very few, if any, shelters because we no longer need them?

I am not saying that you turn your head and let an animal suffer, but you don't need to make it the reality that most, or that many animals suffer. Humans unknowingly respond to the predominant thinking about injustices to animals and even if they love them, they may fall into a category of abusing them, too.

OK, let me get to the solutions! Do you ever wonder why it is so difficult to go to a shelter, why it feels like such a sad place?

I always thought it was because it was like the animals are on death row. When I go in I feel the heaviness, but it really doesn't feel like it is coming from the animals, and in all my communications with them in these situations, I have not heard any of them say that they felt heavy from being there themselves.

You got it! Look, we live in the moment. We truly know that the moment is all there is. We are present with what is going on and we appreciate what we have in the moment. Of course, if we are separated from a human we love, we will miss them, but our main focus is on where we are in the here and now. If we were human we would be terrified because humans fear death and we would truly believe that we are on death row. If we were human, we would be counting down the minutes to our demise and feeling stressful about any possible adoption because if it did not happen, it could be our last chance.

This may sound amazingly confusing! And it may sound crazy for a so-called "victim" to talk in this manner. Let me share the suggested solutions that I hope will perhaps shed more light on the subject.

What we need is love. What humans involved on all sides need is love. They need to care for those animals who need care, but they also need to put their thoughts and focus on the cases where animals are cared for really well. They need to put their focus on the healthy, happy animals. Let's make that the norm — it really is anyway.

What I mean by this is that humans choose the reality they live with. Right now it is crazy with so many causes and that is because of all the drama and all the focus on the problems. It is like the woman you call Mother Teresa. She refused to go to anti-war demonstrations but said if there was a gathering for peace to please invite her.

Humans have been rallying against animal abuse, drugs, war and so many other things. If you truly want to abolish these things, then it is important to work for what you want, rather than fighting against what you don't want.

When you think of abolishing animal abuse and when you fight for this, the truth is you actually create more of it. This is in your thoughts, whether positive or negative, and if it is in your thoughts, it is in your tomorrows, for our tomorrows are created by what you think about today. So instead of creating more shelters, instead of talking about abuse and neglect, let's talk about how to feed an animal, how to work with an animal, how to find the animal that will be compatible for you. Act in ways, and most importantly, THINK in manners that support WHAT YOU APPRECIATE. When you do this, you spend more time thinking about all the happy animals and how wonderfully they are cared for than you do thinking about all the abused ones.

Like I said, it is not that you ignore the abuse, it is that you decide what you want and that you think and act in manners that bring this about. If you talk about and put your focus on the abuse, you are not stopping the problem — you are giving it more power and keeping it alive. Over time, the problem will actually grow bigger and bigger.

Come from a place of love, not fear. When you come from love, you are living in a way that supports what you feel grateful for, what you love. You are thinking about how you would like to see animals cared for. If you are a teacher, you are teaching the joys of feeding and caring for a pet, the joys of having an animal companion, and all the wonderful resources available for our comfort and care. You are not teaching or dwelling on animal abuse, for that only creates a snowball of more and more.

What you feel at the shelters is the fear. It is not the fear of the animals, although we sometimes become afraid of things in the moment. *What you are feeling is the fear of the humans. This fear comes mostly from the masses of people around the world who have their minds honed in on animal abuse. This energy hovers over shelters because they are the location of this intense focus. Some of the employees who work in shelters have the fear as well and they may also feel guilty for somehow being a part of it all.*

It is suggested that when you visit, work in or think of a shelter, you let go of your fear and guilt and instead give whatever love you can. Send love and express love to the animals and the humans. Feel the joy of the human/human connection and the human/animal connection. OK, that was number one!

Number two: I am a very sensitive dog with regard to foods. I am sensitive to ingredients in regular dog food that are not the kind of food a dog would normally eat in the wild. What I am referring to are grains like wheat and corn. Also, I am very sensitive to oils in dog foods as they are often quite old and rancid. Additionally, I am sensitive to other things like peanuts, as you recently found out!

The first day Little Orphan Annie came to live in her new home Elizabeth called me to ask why she was acting so strangely. L.O. Annie asked to be taken to the hospital immediately as she was having a severe reaction to eating something that contained peanuts. It turned out that Elizabeth shared some Thai food leftovers and one was a dish that had peanut sauce.

Little Orphan Annie, please continue your explanation about foods.

When I say that I am "sensitive," I mean along the lines that I will have some sort of reaction when I eat these foods. It might not be noticeable to you, but I will feel it. Sometimes it feels like a drop in energy and other times it feels yucky for awhile until the food is out of my system. I am especially sensitive to gluten proteins that are found in many grains, especially wheat.

Because of my sensitivities, I also would benefit from some probiotics, which are healthy bacteria for my digestive system. Since I ate regular dog food for a period of time and because I am so sensitive and reactive to the ingredients, the healthy bacteria I need for good digestion is deficient in number and in strength.

With a change in diet and some short-term supplementation, I can be at my optimum health in no time! You can ask my doctor (veterinarian) about probiotics or get other suggestions about helping my digestion.

I have some suggestions for my daily diet. A raw or part raw food diet would be best for me. I need raw meats, and some raw vegetables and cooked rice is OK. No noodles! No bread! And, no cheese! No junk food for this dog! I am into health food!

When I say "part raw food diet," I mean that part of the time I could eat some cooked meats, vegetables and rice. Other times I could just eat raw meat and vegetables. I would be happy just eating raw, that would be awesome! Here I have gone from being perceived as a victim to a dog designing her own diet! Yea!

L.O. Annie, do you have any messages for your new human companion?

Yes, I do! Please share this! Dear Woman, I love you so much and I thank you for adopting me into your home and family! Please consider what I have said. I would encourage you to do some research on raw diets for dogs. There are some that you can purchase readymade or you can make your own. Thank you!

Oh, I forgot something! Would you consider another name for me? It is not bad, but I don't think the one I have quite fits. If you think of me in this new way of being a champion, perhaps you will come up with something else. Take your time, I am in no rush. Get to know me in the way that I ask and you will be inspired. Thank you! Love...

When I talked with Elizabeth about Little Orphan Annie's message she agreed to do what she could to begin seeing her dog as a champion as opposed to a victim. She also said she would agree to get to know the dog and allow herself to be inspired by a new name. A few weeks later Elizabeth emailed to tell me she'd chosen the name Grace!

CHAPTER ELEVEN

Albert

M any of my clients contact me by e-mail to explain what they are experiencing with their pets. In the fall of 2003, I received a message from a woman who was obviously very concerned about her dog.

Dear Maia,

My older dog Albert has some kind of physical problem that several veterinarians, including specialists, have not been able to diagnose. He's in a considerable amount of pain, and I give him pain medicine every day. It seems to be his lower back which is involved. Sometimes he limps, favoring his right rear leg. My question is: What is wrong exactly, and what do I need to do to help him? I'll do anything to help him. Please let me know.

Sensing the urgency in her message, I responded as soon as I could and sent her the following e-mail:

I would be happy to check in with your dog, Albert, to see what he is experiencing and how you can help bring him back into healthy balance.

I then quieted myself with a few slow, deep breaths and addressed the dog.

Albert, are you open to communicate?

Yes, of course! I have much that I would like to share with my woman! I adore her!

Albert, would you like to share something about yourself first?

No, I would really like to get right to the point.

Are you in pain?

On and off, but it is mostly just inconvenient.

Go ahead, Albert, what would you like to say to your woman?

My dear Woman, I love you! And I feel so fortunate to be with you sharing this grand adventure. I want you to know that I look worse than I feel; it isn't so bad.

I was bitten by an insect that is affecting my blood and causing me some challenges. Have the doctors check my blood. It is fairly common, but it doesn't usually affect dogs in this way.

Woman, you are afraid of these insects, and you think that they are dangerous with mysterious consequences. My present condition is a physical manifestation of your fears. Our beliefs and fears are generally brought out or manifested in our lives so that we may re-evaluate whether they still serve us by continu-

ing to believe them. We either become stronger in our beliefs and fears or we change our way of seeing things. When we surrender our fears and choose new beliefs, our lives take on an element of adventure as opposed to fear, and we begin to feel a sense of peace that emanates from deep within.

I can be healed. It would help for you to re-examine your beliefs and fears about insects. Don't use my case as a reason to continue believing as you do!

Know that there are many people who never give a second thought to insects; they don't have any fear of them and they have no challenges with them. There are things others fear that you do not fear. They are plagued with challenges where you are not.

Remember that insects are here living their lives just like every other creature. They are not necessarily out to hurt anyone. It is normal to bump into one once in a while and perhaps get bitten. As you know, fear of them attracts them to you so that you have the opportunity to work through that fear. So in order to help me and you, please look at how you view these insects. Begin to develop a love for them. I will recover in time as you develop a peaceful feeling about the little creatures. I love you, dear Woman!

Don't worry! Once I am healed, I won't get this again. I will be immune to it because I have now been immunized. And I am sure the other dogs won't get it. The bite created an infection of sorts which is causing my discomfort. There is some inflammation in my hindquarters causing the challenges with movement, but it will subside in time.

Alternating hot and cold packs on my low back near the spine, just above the pelvis will help relieve some of the discom-

fort and help to clear this out. Thank you! Albert.

I e-mailed Albert's message to his woman and also sent several more after that to be sure she received his message, but did not hear from her for weeks. Finally, I received this message:

Maia,

The reason I have taken so long to respond to Albert's message is that I was very angry when I read it. It is true that I did have paranoia of insects in the past, but I have worked through all that, and it is no longer a problem. I was very angry when Albert said that I am paranoid about insects and I still am irritated about this! I don't think that it is true!

When she hadn't responded, I suspected that there were some issues for her with Albert's message. This is a common occurrence in my work and I have learned not to take this personally or to stress about it. Instead I rely on the animals to sort it out because they know their humans better than anyone. Before responding to Albert's human, I decided to talk with him again to allow him the opportunity to respond to her comments and her anger.

Albert, do you understand your woman's response to the information you shared?

Yes, of course! I have been living with it!

Let me say to my woman that it is true that your achievement of peace in regard to past fears with insects is remarkable! We are delighted and we congratulate you! But there is still one insect that continues to cause you problems.

ALBERT

You have released many fears and brought yourself to a place of contentment and peace that was once not so accessible. In addition to this grand shift within yourself, you have offered a blessing of understanding and love to the magic kingdom of what you call insects. We are very pleased with your work, Woman! As I mentioned though, there is an insect that still elicits a reaction within you. You are encouraged to discover what this insect is and to continue in your work with this creature. If you sit quietly and ask yourself which insect it is, you will know.

Your previous accomplishment in releasing fears of the past will make the release of this fear even simpler now. This is a wonderful accomplishment! It will give you a sense of completeness to your work. Celebrate your accomplishments, Woman. Know that I will respond to your new understandings with vibrant health. You have proven to yourself that you are capable of grand things. Don't forget this!

I e-mailed Albert's message and added this one of my own:

> That was Albert's message! I too, would like to congratulate you on bringing yourself to the place where you are. Coming to a peaceful place in the face of our personal fears can be challenging. According to Albert, you have achieved something quite powerful yet there is one insect that he says still brings out fear in you when you think of it. I would encourage that you sit quietly, as he suggested, and that you ask yourself which insect bit Albert.
>
> Thank you, love to you & your family!
> Maia

DOGS SAY THE DARNDEST THINGS

The next day I received this response in my Inbox:

Maia,

I now know which insect bit Albert — it was a tick. They get on me and my animals. I have protected the animals, but they still sometimes show up. They gross me out! I used to burn them when I found them — yuck. I no longer do this and am working on having compassion for them as well as for all the rest of the creepy-crawlers. It will take some more time. I guess I do have some fear of insect-borne diseases — guess I need to work on resolving that as well!

Many blessings to you, thanks _so_ much for your help.

CHAPTER TWELVE

Truth

Oने of the most important things I have learned with regard to my conversations with people's pets is to do whatever I can to keep an open mind. Over the years, I have experienced many surprises when I questioned animals about their lives and about life in general. While reading and pondering some of the dialogs in this book, perhaps you wondered what it would be like to receive some new information that did not fit with what you thought you knew to be true about yourself or about life.

There have been times during my career as an Animal Communication Specialist when I have literally been shocked by what I heard. In looking back, the thing that's interesting is that these "new" insights usually end up becoming my new insights once I've overcome my resistance to change. The information the animals share makes so much sense, feels so correct and clarifies so much confusion I once had.

I've felt resistance at times to accept and incorporate new information initially because even though I felt its truth, my acceptance of it meant that I had to re-evaluate so many other beliefs that were connected to it. Sometimes it seemed overwhelming! I felt as though I was lifted upside down and shaken and all that I knew and all that I thought was dropped out onto the floor, scattered about in total disorder. At times I simply had to sit with the information and just be and do the basic things in my life that have me feeling grounded and content. Then I could revisit this newly presented truth only while looking at it safely out of the corner of my eye. Later I would be ready to look at it head on and allow the files of my understanding to reorder themselves based on this new piece of information.

Whenever I go through the process of embracing a new truth it's always much easier than I think it will be at first to bring myself together — new understanding and all — because in time, the new information really resonates with me.

It seems like once I surrender and relax with the new information I have received, everything literally jumps into place in my mind as so many mistaken beliefs are naturally and easily left behind. I've always felt so much more peaceful and come away with a greater level of understanding once I have fully embraced the concepts I've received. It's as if all the questions in my mind and heart are gradually being cleared up through conversations with dogs and other beings of Nature.

There have been times where I wanted information for myself from a particular animal or species and they refused to talk with me, saying that I was not ready to receive it. There have been times where I felt anger and frustration because I believed that I was being jerked around by what seemed like double talk. In looking back on a lifetime of receiving mentorship from Nature, including and especially with dogs, I must say it's been an amazing journey and I wouldn't change a thing! Today I feel deeply grateful. The information I have received has literally transformed my life (when I put it into practice). Every so often I get a reminder that I need to live what I've learned. I'll never forget a conversation I had with some medicinal plants that asked if I minded if they went off topic to talk about my eating habits. They then proceeded to rag on me for eating as though I was a vacuum cleaner and gave me positive suggestions for change. I'm still working on it!

My clients often receive information for themselves that surprises them as well. Many comment on how they've managed to change their lives in a wonderful way by simply following the advice of their pet. We humans often carry unnecessary guilt and are sometimes confused with regard to our beloved pets. We care so deeply for them that we also tend to have powerful emotions in relation to them and their lives. A conversation with a pet has the potential to clear up many erroneous beliefs, offering peace and healing to both the human and the animal. I've experienced incredibly precious and powerful moments with clients and their pets, where for example, their dog has shared its truth and the human has embraced it, releasing long-held mistaken beliefs that pained them both.

I have also experienced working with humans who have requested that I tell their animal to stop a particular behavior. I came to find out they had no interest in why the animal behaved as it did, neither did they have any interest in finding a solution that made everyone happy — they simply wanted me to tell their pet to stop the behavior. I cannot tell an animal how to behave any more than I can tell a fellow human how to behave. All I can do is find out why an animal is behaving the way it is and whether there is a message reflected in the behavior that they wish to convey to their human. I can ask if the animal is at all willing to change its actions and if so, what is required for that to happen. Sometimes the animal will have a list of simple yet important requests. Sometimes they don't like their name and feel that in order to change the undesirable behavior, (which coincidently often fits the name they were given) they need a new name that reflects the kind of behavior their human desires. Some clients respond angrily to the information; they argue that it is not true and refuse to consider taking any action on the simple requests of their dog. Other clients may experience both anger and resistance but don't want to talk about it with me.

These situations can be distressing for me because it seems so easy to bring harmony to a household if the human would only take responsibility for their part in the challenge, and take action to change. I have felt my own resistance at times to heed the wise suggestions of animals and change things in my life, so I do understand that part of the challenge.

I am very fortunate that most of my clients are referrals from other clients or people who've heard about and understand my work. It is a joy to work with them because they really do want to hear their pets and in communicating with them my client and I learn so many things from their animals that enrich our lives. These clients tend to be seeking answers for higher awareness, so they're open to looking at themselves and making the simple changes their animals request which often brings greater joy to them as well as to their pet. Most often, when an animal has a change in behavior, they are attempting to alert us to something important. It could be a change in the status of their health or our health, but usually it is a message for us because they are concerned that we are wandering off our path and they sincerely want to help bring us back into alignment with our goals, our passion and our joy.

When I'm asked to talk with a dog about a new behavior, I like to get to know the dog first by simply taking a few breaths while I pause to give them my attention. When we pause like this we join as one and I am able to feel their personality and way of being. Then I begin asking questions about the behavior, their level of contentment, and any messages for or requests of their human. Sometimes the dogs will go to great lengths to describe themselves before they respond to the questions about their behavior. Other dogs will get right to the point and talk about what's on their mind and in their hearts.

A few years ago I was contacted by a client named Rebecca whom I've known for three or four years. She wanted some assistance in understanding a new and troubling behavior with her dog Billie, who I'd talked with on a few occasions in the past. Here is Rebecca's email to me describing Billie's behavior:

Dear Maia,

I am having a challenge with my dog Billie. I have taken her to work with me for a number of years now, but lately when I arrive she refuses to get out of my truck. I literally have to pull her out so that we can go into the office. I don't want to force her, but I need to get to work. Will you check with her to see why she is behaving this way?

Thanks Maia,
Rebecca

I took a few moments to clear my mind so that I could be fully present to talk with Billie, who was a wise and wonderful dog and a loving companion to Rebecca.

Hello Billie, how are you feeling?

Hello Woman, I am feeling fine! My reason for not wanting to get out of the truck is not due to any health challenge. It is simply that my woman does not want to go into the office so I don't want to go in either. I feel her lack of desire to go and I stand by what I feel she feels.

Billie, what do you suggest?

I suggest that we do something fun instead. I want to go where my woman wants to go. I want to do what my woman wants to do! I feel that she does not want to go into the office.

But Billie, what if she really needs to go into the office?

Then I suggest that she decides she wants to go! I suggest that somehow she changes the way she looks at it so that she wants to go; otherwise, I will continue to resist going in. I don't have a problem with going into the office, she does.

Thank you, Billie! I will share your message with your woman. I sent an email to Rebecca and received the following response: Maia, it is true that I have not wanted to go into the office lately. Wow, Billie is amazing, isn't she!

I replied:

Yes, Rebecca, she certainly is!

A week later I received another email from Rebecca about Billie's behavior.

Maia,

Billie is getting out of the truck fine now at work. But, yesterday I arrived at my house in the evening and she refused to get out. I asked myself how I was feeling and what was going on and I realized that I didn't want to go home because I had some family visiting. They were getting into my personal life, and I really did not want to go home and deal with them. As soon as I realized that I didn't want to go in the house, I took some deep breaths and worked with myself to change my attitude and face what I needed to face. Billie hopped out of the truck and ran to the door. Billie is getting out of the truck just fine now! Thanks Maia! Please thank Billie, too.

It is a great pleasure to work with clients like Rebecca and dogs like Billie! Our lives are so closely intertwined with those of our beloved pets that it's no wonder we can learn so much from them.

The animals often talk about choosing to live with their particular humans for purposes that align with their own interests and agendas. They often choose us based on compatibility of lifestyle, but sometimes they choose a human who doesn't seem to "fit" with them so well. In these cases a dog's behavior or manner of being might push their human to develop more patience or understanding, or to work through some fear they have.

People often ask me to talk with animals they are thinking about adopting into their family. I frequently receive emails with lists of the names of dogs or horses or I'll be given the names over the phone. I will talk with each animal on the list and feel each one's personality as we talk. They generally know why I have been asked to talk with them and they seem to know the human who is interested in adopting them, even when they haven't met them in person.

To give you an example, I might have a man ask me to talk with a group of horses living in various regions of the United States whom he himself has not met; he's only seen either photos or videos of them. Despite what we may assume is an inability to connect, these horses know the man well and know without question whether they would like to join him to be his horse or not. The same is true of a group of dogs; they really let you know what their interests are and whether the human in question will be a good match for them. There is as much variety in the personalities and interests of dogs as there is in humans. I always find it interesting to hear what pets have to say about their prospective humans and how specific they can be in their own selection process. Here we believe we are choosing a pet while in truth, the pet has already carefully evaluated us and the appropriateness of our coming together with them to be a family.

A few years ago I had the pleasure to converse with some greyhounds who were transitioning from a career in racing to

new lives as family pets. After much consideration, my new client Janet had decided to adopt a greyhound. The circumstances of the adoption required that she choose a dog without having the opportunity to meet him or her in person. Janet was given the names of three dogs and some basic details about their ages and temperaments. I was asked to talk with each of them to see if they had any insight into this important choice for Janet and possibly for themselves.

When I have a list of animal's names, I either allow the animals to decide who will talk first or I keep to a list. In this case there were only three dogs, so I decided to just let them know I was available to talk. I immediately felt the presence of a warm and loving dog named Samantha. She could not contain her enthusiasm and her desire to speak. Samantha was intently focused and knew just what she wanted. She felt unusually calm to me for an animal who had lived her life as a finely-tuned racing dog. I liked her instantly and felt the kind of rapport I feel when I meet a human who immediately feels like a kindred spirit and an instant friend.

Samantha knew exactly what she wanted — she wanted Janet to be her human. She was ready to embark on a new life and felt very excited about exploring a loving relationship with Janet. Samantha felt so genuine to me and so stable. I asked how she knew she would like Janet as her human. She indicated that she just knew; she felt Janet through me even though I did not really know Janet myself. She also got to know Janet by Janet's thoughts of her. Samantha explained that whenever we think of someone, they end up thinking of us and we can get to know a lot by just taking a few moments to feel another's energy.

The next dog I talked with was Hally, and it was as if I was talking with her while she was in the midst of many other activities and fleeting thoughts. She felt scattered and excited and excitable to me. She was very sweet, but had no idea what she wanted, nor had she come to understand that her career in racing had come to an end. She was just in the moment, ready for whatever came along. When I asked Hally if she was interested in being adopted by Janet, she said she really wasn't sure, and once again I had the sense that she was busy with many other things and not really fully present. This was an unusual experience for me because generally, dogs are keenly aware and present in their conversations and I have received numerous helpful suggestions and tips from dogs to enhance my listening and communicating skills over the years.

The last of the three dogs was Smart Alec, who let me know immediately that she was a trickster and that she was well named. Like Hally, Smart Alec was very active and engaged with other things as we spoke, but unlike Hally, Smart Alec really liked her name and had a sense of pride in her reputation of pushing the buttons of the humans around her. When I asked her about being Janet's pet, she showed very little interest, almost ignoring my question altogether. She did not have a strong pull to be with my client and like Hally, was just waiting to see what would come along.

During this conversation, in addition to getting a feel for the personalities and wishes of the dogs, Janet and I looked in on their health, including past injuries. It was important to sense which dog was most likely to love her new life with this particular woman. But before I finished, Samantha joined me once again and reinforced her passion about having a life with Janet. I felt Samantha's excitement and I felt happiness for Janet and her great fortune to have a new, loving companion.

A few months later, Janet shared her experience of adopting Samantha. She was sitting in a crowded room of people when out came a greyhound dog who ran right past her and never came to say hello. This was Hally. Then Samantha came bounding out into the large room, went directly to Janet and stayed with her until all the details were worked out to take her home. Janet joyfully shared the news of her love for Samantha and how well they were settling into their new life together.

It is interesting that we might make a different decision in choosing a dog if we don't take the time to talk with them directly about who they are and want they want. Before I began communicating directly with animals, asking questions in the way that I do today, I assumed many things that ultimately have proved to be incorrect. I have also opened my mind to the fact that, based on what I know as a human, I may not automatically know the needs or desires of an animal. I have come to realize and notice that we humans make a lot of assumptions about other species — we believe we know what they want, who they are, and how they think. We generally do this based on our love for them and our concerns for their comfort, but also from our desire to feel a sense of control with regard to their care and well-being.

The places and situations where I've probably been most surprised and enlightened have been in conversations either with animals living in shelters or in transition to a new home or with those involved in the transition of death. Sometimes I visit shelters to talk with animals in an effort to learn more about what they think about being in transition. Like many of us, before I began to ask questions of animals, I assumed I knew how the experience was for them, based on how I thought it would be for me if I was an animal. Since my first visit to a shelter, though, I've learned that much of what I assumed to be true was not. Each dog is different, just as each human is different, so I have learned to keep an open mind in order to really listen to the individual to understand what they want for themselves.

Once, some years ago I visited a kennel and was asked by a dog to be adopted. Wow, did that tug at my heart! I was coming from the standpoint of feeling so bad to see so many animals in the shelter and not in loving homes. I explained to the dog that I had just returned from being out of the country and planned to leave again soon. I said that it wasn't practical and seemed unfair to begin a new life with an animal when I wasn't planning to be living here. He then proceeded to give me a dissertation about how we humans try to think ahead too much, how we should be a little more spontaneous and that I should just adopt him and see how life unfolds. He assured me that being together could be magic even if it only lasted a few months — it would be worth it.

That day however, I could not get around all my preconceived ideas and celebrate a short relationship with this wonderful dog, so despite his great sales pitch, I did not adopt him. It turned out that he knew something I didn't because I didn't leave the country again and he and I could have enjoyed a life together, but I was too uncertain about my upcoming future and I thought I knew what I was doing. He definitely put my mind and heart in a jumble and I still appreciate how speaking with him set me on a path of opening my mind and heart even more to understanding the real truth. (Fortunately, he ended up being adopted by someone who really was looking for a dog and they formed a warm and playful bond with one another.)

On another visit to a shelter, I paused in a long row of kennels filled with dogs awaiting adoption and listened to one of them say, "Don't even think about it!" When I asked what he meant he said, "Don't even think about adopting me." Baffled, I asked why and he explained that he had other plans and needed to make the transition of death in order to get where he was going. He went on to say that he had a dream of being a different type of dog and wanted to have a different experience of life. He wanted to be an athlete and to train and perform in close harmony with a human.

I've also talked with animals who actually wanted their humans to take them to a shelter or what some of them call "The Marketplace", so they could find another human. In cases like this, the two were incompatible and neither the dog nor the person was particularly happy about their life together. But out of a sense of guilt, the person planned to keep the dog, despite their lack of joy. Dogs in this position often plead with their human to please take them to a shelter so they may "shop" for "their" human, someone they will be happier with. They think of going to the shelter as a good thing and they're eager to get there so they can begin to look for a new human and a new life.

Then there are dogs who feel very stressed being in a shelter who don't want to stay, and others who don't even want a new home. A few years ago I visited a no-kill animal shelter in northern Arizona where I met a little dog named Rose. She was very tiny and fine-boned for a dog of 14 months and she looked like no other dog I had ever seen — maybe a little Shepherd, but I wasn't sure what else. Actually, the more I looked at her, the more she looked like she was part coyote. Rose had a sweet inquisitive expression that longed for connection. She had been picked up off the Navajo Indian Reservation where she had been found running with a pack of dogs.

Little Rose indeed confirmed that she was part coyote, part Shepherd and part she was not sure what. She had been raised by a family on a ranch where she lived out of doors, running free. She loved her life with her humans on the reservation and found no stress in it, other than the ride in when she was brought to the shelter. This was really unpleasant for her because she had never traveled in a vehicle before and was unsettled by the movement.

Rose hoped that she could just return to her former life of freedom, but she was also open to connecting with humans and was curious about what we were all about. Rose's mind and heart were amazingly open to us. She said she was not afraid and that her humans on the reservation were kind to her. She confided to me that she asked each human who passed her kennel to get her out of there. She did not care where as long as they just put her outside somewhere. She was confident that she could fend for herself. She said she loved to hunt and especially liked little burrowing animals, but that she would also jump at birds flying overhead too, especially when they pestered her.

I asked Rose how she ended up there. She responded that she left her home on the reservation with some other dogs who had wandered in and that she was having fun playing and running with them. It never occurred to her that she was leaving or that she would end up in a shelter. She explained that a human driving a truck stopped and put out some boxes (sounded like crates to me) with meat in them. Naturally, she and her companions dove into the boxes, but could not get out. They were then all lifted into the truck and that was when Rose had the uncomfortable experience of movement.

So Rose, what is it that you really want now?

To get out of here!

Would you be interested in living in a home with humans?

Not really — it is hard to imagine. That would be a new experience for me. I really want to run free again. It is possible that I could like living in a house, but I don't know. I am very sweet and kind. I would not hurt anyone.

Rose, do you have a message for humans?

Yes, I would like to point out that what you might think of as an unpleasant situation for one of us animals could be entirely different for another. For instance, I loved my life. I was so content and I felt so alive. I want to return to it. Now I feel like I am being punished, but the humans who picked me up and those here at the shelter really believe that I was abused and abandoned and that now I am being taken care of. In my opinion I was being cared for before and now I am in prison. Sure, I get food regularly and the humans are so loving and kind, but I am in a cage. I cannot play with my friends or go off wandering as I wish.

I realize that for some animals this level of freedom might not work and that many animals have other desires, but please just take into consideration that some of us might like it the way it is. This does not need to stop you from taking me or another in, but it can give you a new outlook on the situation that might help you work with us. I am grateful for this experience, but I do long for my freedom. I don't mind being spayed, but I would love to run free again. Maybe we could all be brought in and neutered and then put back out on the reservation again. Thank you for listening.

You are welcome Rose!

Years ago I wouldn't have guessed that Rose would want to be back on the reservation running free; I might have actually believed she'd been "rescued" from there. But today, after all I've heard in 13 years of communicating with people's pets, her response does not surprise me. And I can understand it — living on the reservation with her family was a good life for her.

I decided to check back with Rose telepathically a few months after we'd met to see how she was doing. It turned out that she had been adopted as a pet for a shy young twelve-year-old girl. At first, Rose was overwhelmed with all the attention she received and she kept looking for a way to wander, but soon her focus began to change as she fully joined her young human in forming a beautiful bond between them. In hindsight she admitted that she loved her life — all of it — including her days of wandering free as a bird with her Native American family, and now living as a pet for a young girl. Even her time at the shelter was not so bad with all the care she received. She expressed her gratitude and joy which brought a smile to my face.

It's always wonderful when we can experience a happy ending like this, but sometimes we humans may not think a happy ending is possible or likely. We tend to believe that a dog must possess certain characteristics in order to be adopted. Perhaps these ideas came from studies or from trends in animal adoption. It is possible, however, that we've gone too far in labeling a pet as a problem to the point where we actually hinder the adoption process. One case that comes to mind is a medium-sized mixed breed dog who I met the same day I met Rose.

I'll let her speak for herself!

My name is Sophie. You met me at the shelter. I want to say that I am considered to be an aggressive dog because I speak loudly and regularly and with assertiveness. It is often taken as being aggressive and perhaps danger-ous. I startle people with my frankness and it has brought me here to live at the shelter. For the most part, I am well understood by the humans here at the shelter. They treat me kindly and have overcome their initial fear of me — I admit my style is intimidating.

The shelter humans want to place me in a home, but they are concerned about whether other humans will feel intimidated by my brash manner. I feel their concern, which in turn makes

175

me feel a bit nervous and on edge. It is a recipe for failure when dogs are on edge and feeling like we could make a mistake. I know that I pose a challenge and I understand that it may be stressful for the humans here who so want me to find a new home. This is what they call a no-kill shelter so they will keep me until I do find a home, but after a great while if I prove to be a behavioral problem, they could take action to eliminate me.

OK, here is my message: I feel deeply grateful to these humans here at the shelter. I understand the challenges that I pose for them with my particular personality. But let us look at this realistically. I have passed the safety tests. I have not bitten, nor do I plan to bite or harm anyone in any way. I think the shelter humans are really sure about this.

The thing is that they continue to see my behavior as a challenge and they continue to feel stress about it. They talk about me amongst themselves, building more and more stress on this topic and even when they are alone, they continue to talk in their heads about my difficult behavior.

All of this is fear, and it creates a lot of stress for the humans at the shelter, for me and for any prospective humans who might consider adopting me to one day be their dog. So, I ask my humans at the shelter and other humans out there in similar situations to please work through your fears. Face your own individual fears. Ask yourself what you will do if this or if that happens. Then, simply accept that this is all you can do and put it into the hands of what is in the highest good for all those involved. You carry too much responsibility on your shoulders and it causes stress all around.

When you hold onto all of your worries about me, it is as

if you put a dark cloud over me. It makes it more stressful and difficult for me to be me — my real self. It is hard on you, and ultimately it supports an unfavorable outcome. If you stop thinking that you need to figure out what you are going to do in case I don't change or if someone does not find me compatible, you can release this and trust that it will either work out one way or another. All you can do is relax and enjoy relating with me. Share with visitors openly about my challenges and allow people coming in to make up their own minds and see what happens. We are not trying to fool anyone here! I want to be my real self with my humans and they need to see how they feel with me, so please remove the dark cloud of your own fears from me so that I can make my own way. Please turn your love and concern into something good for us all. Relax! You do so many wonderful things already. Let me fly! I have faith that I can find some boisterous humans who like to talk a lot and who talk fast and loud. We can have a party! Thank you!

Ultimately, Sophie was adopted by a man who was looking for a canine to accompany him in his retirement. He was a little hard of hearing so her strong voice was of benefit to him and he really appreciated her bossy, bold personality. She became his adoring friend and went right to work, lovingly guiding him in her care and their adventures together.

CHAPTER THIRTEEN
Melissa

I was enjoying the crisp mountain air of the early morning as I checked my e-mail and looked over my schedule. The first conversation of the day was to be with a dog named Melissa. Before talking with her, I decided to re-read the e-mail I received from her human to remind me of her particular situation.

Hello Maia,

I would like to ask you some questions about my daughter's dog, Melissa. She is an eight-year-old black Labrador. For the past few years, she has had what seem to be seasonal allergies. She often has skin challenges and she loses a lot of her hair. She looks pitiful and I worry about her. Will you talk with her and see how we can help?

After rereading the message, I paused for a few moments to center myself and then began to talk with the dog.

Melissa, do you have some information for your humans as to how they can help you with the challenges you are having?

First, let me say that my humans are challenged more than I am, and that what they see in me is an overflow of what they are dealing with. Let me explain. I am a very happy dog and, for the most part, I am in good health. What is going on here is a situation where one human is trying to help the other and the other does not want to be helped. I have chosen to tangle myself in this web. Let me say that I tell you this with a smile on my face as I chose this knowingly and lovingly. How often do you see a Labrador with little or no hair? This is not the normal hairstyle of my kind! But I chose it to express a message.

Basically, my woman has a man in her life that my woman's mother does not like. Mother tries and tries to get along and to be supportive, but underneath she is concerned. The mother of my woman thinks of the challenges of the relationship her daughter is in, and she understands that somehow her daughter chose this, but she then puts her attention into fearing for me. She thinks about how toxic the environment is for me, the poor dog! So, I respond to this thinking by showing her that indeed, she is correct — just look at me with no hair! It really is a sad situation! In reality, I am fine. I don't like the young man either, but I can deal with this. Meanwhile, my woman is unconcerned and fails to look at her relationship with this man to really evaluate it, because she senses that her mother is doing lots of evaluating for her.

My suggestion to the mother is that she truly accepts her daughter's choice and that she gives up trying to change the

*situation by coming from a place of trying to protect "the dog".
Instead, I recommend that she just let the whole thing go and
put her attention on living her own life more fully, passionately
and joyfully. When she lets my woman go, totally respecting her
choice, then my woman will feel the responsibility of her own life
more fully in her own hands and she will then be more likely to
make many changes in her life, perhaps even choosing a partner
who has greater respect and appreciation for her. I am fine either
way. I will wear my rough coat as an expression or I will allow
my shimmering, brilliant black coat to stand out at last. No matter what they choose, I love my humans!*

Melissa, what is it that makes a dog continue to love their
humans no matter what? You must be uncomfortable when you
are itching and scratching and losing your hair due to these human challenges.

*The bottom line is that we animals love our humans. Our
love is like that of a parent who loves a child no matter what
mistakes he or she makes. We have a wonderful sense of humor
as well. We love to laugh and we like to make light of what we
can. In addition, we fear very little if anything, even what you
humans term to be death. We have nothing to lose so we delve
deeply into our lives and deeply into our experience. We live
fully in the moment, embracing all that we have.*

Thank you, Melissa!

Thank you, Woman!

CHAPTER FOURTEEN

Boy & Dog

Some of my animal communication students are children. I work with them on a weekly basis by telephone just like I do with my adult students. Rather than teaching them, I like to think that I am "reminding" my students. I simply give guidance, structure and encouragement to the awakening of their innate abilities. I believe that all humans have the ability to communicate with Nature as I do and it is my passion to help as many people as possible experience the delight of conversing with our fellow beings of life.

A few weeks ago I received an e-mail from a woman writing for her son who had questions for his dog. She asked for a consultation as opposed to a class, so in this case I talked with the dog and passed along the information to be shared with the boy. In a class, my students and I ask an animal questions together so that the students can gain experience and confidence in their listening skills, whereas in a consultation, I converse with the animal

and share the information with his or her humans. Here is the
e-mail I recently received:

Dear Maia,

I would like to request an animal communication consultation for my son so that he will have greater understanding
with his dog, Sarah. My son actually only has a few questions. Kids are so simple, it's wonderful!
  Sarah is a 3-year old Welsh springer spaniel. My son is
13 years old. He would like to ask Sarah why she has a hard
time sitting still while being petted.

Shortly after receiving this message, I made an appointment
to talk with Sarah. Before we connected, I sat quietly and surrendered other thoughts and plans so that my mind was uncluttered.
I took a few slow, deep breaths and I noted how wonderful it felt
to just be. Then I simply greeted her.

Hello, Sarah!

Hello, Woman!

Sarah, your young human has some questions for you. But
before we begin, would you tell me about yourself?

*I am colorful in all ways! I am playful. I am usually eager to
greet strangers, but when I slow down I pay more attention and
sometimes I'm a little shy. I am like a little girl! I am so happy!
I love this human child soooo much! I am so excited to be loved
by him that I have a hard time being still! I feel so happy and
have so much love that I can hardly contain myself.*

Young Man, if you imagine me being still it will help me to be that way. Please don't imagine or think that I have a problem. Remember that I love you and I will work to be still. But it will help me if you will imagine me sitting still while you pet me. You can help me learn to relax by thinking of me sitting and being very peaceful yourself while you gently pet me. Take a few deep, slow, relaxing breaths and you will help me to settle down and breathe, too.

Sarah, your young human would like to know if you love him the most. He has some confusion about that because you were his older brother's dog at first.

Please let me explain. I love all of you but I know that I am your dog and that you are my human. In that way we have our own special love because we are partners in a sense.

Sarah, your human thinks that you are funny and he wonders whether you have a sense of humor and if you laugh. He laughs a lot at things you do, and really likes you snuggling with him and how you get under the covers.

You knew I was laughing, and you were correct. I laugh all the time and I like to do things to make you laugh! That is what life is all about! It brings me great joy to be with you and to hear your laughter, to see your smile and to feel those warm feelings of love in your heart! I think it is good for both of us. I feel so good when you and I laugh! You are very funny, too!

Sarah, he says that you drive him crazy the way that you constantly stare at him. He wants to know what you want. Is it food? I heard that you were obsessed with food and that you are insatiable for bones from the grocery store. Your human also says that he would like to take you places, but that you are so crazy and uncontrollable.

I must admit that I like those bones and would always love another but also I stare at you because I want you to know how much I love you. I want you to love and appreciate yourself, young man. I feel so grateful to have you as my human and to be with your wonderful family. When I stare at you, I am expressing my deep love for you and I am asking you to notice how wonderful you are, too.

I am playful and silly and it seems like I cannot be still for a second unless I am sound asleep. I am quite peaceful inside and I would enjoy sharing this peace and some wisdom with you if you would like to listen. All that you have to do, young man, is take a few moments when you can sit quietly yourself, take a deep breath and perhaps you will pick up some words that express my love for you. It is my wish that you go on laughing, that you really enjoy your life.

Let me say a few things about how you can help me learn to walk on a leash and be easier to control so that we can go everywhere. I ask that you practice very simple things at first. I can only pay attention for a few seconds and then I am distracted thinking about other things. Begin by calling my name quietly to get me focused. Oh, but first take a breath so that you relax and so you are paying attention, too. Then, imagine that I am sitting very quietly and ask me to sit. Be very gentle and help me to sit when you ask. Next, you can ask me to walk on the leash for just a few steps and then let's sit again.

What I am saying here is that you and I can only be serious for a few moments and then we will get playful. But we can practice for a few minutes and then we can play. After some practice, we will be able to walk quietly for more and more moments and we will be able to start going many places together. It is best to start practicing in a small, quiet area. As we improve in our ability to focus, we can go to bigger and bigger places with more and more distractions because we will have this peaceful practice to keep us calm and safe.

I only beg for food when I see you eating it, or when I smell food and I know you will eat it soon.

Sarah, you feel like a very sweet and trusting dog. Your humans would like to help you so that you can do things together with them. Do you have anything else you would like to share?

When I stare at you, I am asking that you pause and quiet your mind. Think of something you would like to do with me, such as going outside and walking around the house. In your mind, imagine going out the door with me and walking around the house together. Don't say a word in your human language, and don't touch me. Once you have imagined this, get up and walk to the door. I will follow, but if I am reluctant don't say a word, just feel love in your heart and hold the door open for me as you go out. We can do many things together. Try communicating in this way sometimes.

Thank you, Sarah!

Thank you, Woman!

CHAPTER FIFTEEN

Companions in Life

I converse with dogs and cats on a daily basis because they are my clients' most common pets. I enjoy talking with other animals, plants, and insects too, whenever I have the opportunity. Sometimes I put out a request to a particular species to share whatever message they wish and a number of years ago, I put that request out to wolves. I thought it would be interesting to have some insight from them, the wild relative of our dear companion, the dog. What follows is the message the wolves shared.

Dearest Humans, we truly are your companions in life, and in spirit! The relationship between humans and wolves is quite ancient, with its roots originating in the early breaths of human existence.

An understanding of our profound and intertwined history is rare in the minds of humans today due to both the great changes that have occurred, and to the antiquity of our original relationship. Despite these obstacles, this unique bond lives on in the cellular memory of wolves and humans alike.

The mystique of wolf and man is perpetuated by the unexplained rustling of the human spirit in response to thoughts of our species. We feel a profound connection to humans as well.

Today the relationship between wolf and human continues mostly in dreams and in visions. Some humans are inspired to view and also to wear our images. They feel pleasure in knowing our freedom, in turn sensing it themselves through the deep spiritual connection that exists between our species. We encourage humans to call forth the wisdom of our original relationship, for it truly is one of respect and cooperation.

The ancient times of which we speak came long before what you term to be your current times, and long before we as wolves became feared and asked to leave from the territories thought to belong to man.

We have no anger toward humans for attempting to eliminate our species and we did not, nor do we fear the end of our kind. We understand that a human lack of attention to the Divine substance of all life intricately connected leads to ignorance and sometimes to the desire to eliminate other beings of life purely for the desire to do so. What we felt and continue to feel is sadness at the denial of the beauty of our relationship of mutual respect with humans. If you look back on the history of the spirit of relating between wolves and man, you will sense the profound depths of relating that is possible and the opportunities that have always been there for the evolution of understanding of life. All you have to do is look at the precious manner in which humans relate to their dogs to gather a sense of the respect available between wolf and man.

What we see as most important for humanity at this time is the conflict amongst humans themselves and the denial of the connection that runs so strongly between the individuals of your species no matter what color, or size, what God, or what homeland. This truly is the issue; we wolves would not expect to be treated with respect when there is difficulty giving proper respect to the individuals of your own species.

We wolves represent a unique energy in the psyche of the human, a physical manifestation which stands for freedom, confidence, cooperation of family and community, living in alignment with the highest good for the species, and balance with all others. In addition, we represent respect, honor, and a belief to live intently each precious moment, and of course, passion for the experience of life itself.

We find it interesting that with the near elimination of our species by humans that the battle amongst humans to maintain the qualities we represent including integrity, freedom, cooperation, balance, respect, honor, community, and passion for life itself has become heightened, and it appears that the values of humankind are threatened as never before.

We wish to state that we are here to assist in maintaining these qualities by firmly representing what we stand for and what we know that humanity stands for. So despite being sent away, we have not left. We are with you! We are at your side!

As your faithful companions, loyal supporters of the truth, and of life on our Mother Earth, we stand with you in regaining your sense of value, your respect, your integrity, your honor, your confidence, and your passion for living.

We would like to talk about these qualities, for we feel your

confusion and your stress. What seems to be at the root of this
is the choice you humans make to live in fear. Fear is the most
destructive energy to all the families of life, to our Mother Earth,
and ultimately to humankind.

We invite you to join us as we remind you about the true
nature of fear, and we wish to share our understanding of what
we prefer to term "healthy caution."

Imagine an individual member of our species traveling
in a wooded valley. Think of the attentive awareness that is
maintained in each step, in each pause. We wolves are highly
aware of our surroundings and our sense of connectedness to all,
especially to our Mother Earth who directs our needs and assists
in guiding our movements.

We live very intently in the moment, but this does not mean
that we are stressed or that we live in fear. Our attentive awareness reflects our passion for the experience of life itself. We are
quite relaxed and peaceful despite the fact that we are aware of
all that is occurring in and around us.

We do feel what we call healthy caution at times; when we
hear a strange sound, when we smell something peculiar, or we
feel a sudden change in our Mother Earth. At those times, our
awareness is heightened even more. We can zoom in on what
it is and take a really close look, but at the same time maintain
focus on all else as well.

In these moments of heightened awareness, we either stay
in one place or we run, depending on what we sense. Then we
quickly return to our relaxed, peaceful, yet ever-so-wakeful state.

When we return to our normal attentive state, we have
released any tension from what was felt in that previous moment

of heightened awareness. We do not carry what humans term to be stress, nor do we feel stress all the time, as many humans do. We keep past memories for the purpose of learning, to assist individual wolves and our species as a whole in the continuation of life. We do not hold onto emotions, nor do we continue to react to them again and again over time.

It is our observation that many humans today live in constant fear of one thing or another. There also appears to be a lack of attentiveness or awareness of the present moment, a lack of self-awareness, and both a lack of awareness of one's relationship with another and with the Earth. Perhaps all this is the cause of the fear?

We would like to remind you that when you are fearful, you are generally not living in the moment, but in what you term to be the future or the past.

Put in simple terms, it is our observation that many humans live in an artificial manner, cut off from the Divine wisdom of nature that is waiting to be utilized. In this state of supposed separation, there is confusion. Actions are taken based on the good of a few rather than on the good of all life, without understanding that acting based on the good of only a few members of a species threatens the survival of the species as a whole.

We say these things not to arouse more fear, but to remind you that each one of you dear beings has a deep wisdom within that can be called upon at all times. We wolves live in alignment with this Divine wisdom in all moments. That is why we are so delighted in our experience, for each moment is so rich and we desire to experience each moment fully by utilizing all of our senses.

For us, it is a matter of the continuation of ourselves as individuals and of the existence of our species. We are constantly being tested to keep our senses honed and to understand the environment in which we live, which includes the human consciousness. This does not mean that we live in fear, for we do not.

We live in alignment with the wisdom of Nature, which is a sense of peace, appreciation for the preciousness of each moment, and the certain knowledge of the continuity of life.

What we are suggesting here, dear humans, is that each one of you look deeply within yourselves to align with your highest wisdom. This can be done just as we do it, by living fully present in all your moments. If you are walking, pay attention to your walking and to all that you sense in and around you. Imagine that you are a wolf. How attentive would you be in your life? In these fully attentive moments you will find peace and you will find the pure joy of being, or of doing even the most mundane task.

This is where you will find patience and the understanding of more profound understandings, bringing you to even greater peace within yourself and within your species. This is where you will find support for the foundation of your existence by feeling grounded in your Mother Earth as we are, and you will have no need for fear as you now know it.

We suggest that you practice being entirely present in each moment. Can you imagine one of us wolves walking along thinking about something we did yesterday? It is not a common practice, and in fact, it is perhaps entirely unknown to our kind.

If you are present in the moment, whether it be walking along a river, or talking to one of your cubs, you will feel the wisdom of nature that exists within all beings of life and you

194

no need to worry about us, we're fine because we have a never-ending source of love coming into us. We simply want to invite you humans to join us so that you too, can feel the joy of simply being without all the desperation, struggle and strife of gathering your energy from your environment.

Orson, why do you say "even and especially insects"?

That is because I know your species in general has little appreciation for ......

What's going on Orson?

Well, I'm having difficulty explaining something because the human species is so far removed in its understanding of insects that I don't know where to begin. This is a whole topic of its own and that is not my purpose here today, so let me just say that there is so much more going on in the realm of insects and life than what is known to humans. On some levels, insects can annoy even a dog, but the truth is they are very important beings in the scheme of life. They are highly attuned to the breath and they like dogs and other beings of life are always filled to the brim with Divine love and light and with the wisdom that naturally comes with the breath.

Orson, will you talk about Divine love and light so that we might understand what you mean by this?

Divine love and light is the spark that resides within all beings of life. It is what births you into life in the first place and what feeds and nurtures your Divine body, mind and spirit throughout your life. All species and individuals of life have full will feel instinctively aligned with what is in the highest good for your species, your family, and your community. For when you are fully present in the moment, that is all that exists; it is precious, and it is most often peaceful.

With a new/old habit of living in this manner, you will know and live by your values without question. You will be respectful of your own dear being, your species and all families of life, and you will feel the preciousness of each breath, each moment of this experience you call life. This is our wish for you, dear humans!

We invite you to join us once again in this magnificent dance of life. Whether you relate with us in a physical sense or not, is not of great importance compared to regaining the qualities that are at your roots, and at the roots of our relationship with you. We are here at your side in your dreams and in your visions. Call on us in your slumber and in your days. Ask us to guide you in walking in awareness, in being alert, peaceful, and joyfully alive!

CHAPTER SIXTEEN
Kanoe

When I met Kanoe, I was living on a ranch on the east side of the Cascade Mountain range in Oregon. My home was situated on the divide between the foothills of the Cascade Mountains and the beginning of the high desert that makes up most of the state. I loved the location as it afforded ample opportunity for adventures into the arid desert region to the east, or I could travel west into the mountains of the Cascades. It was a fascinating landscape rich in opportunity for exploration. I had the sense of feeling small in the midst of a large pool of endless possibility with no worries about becoming saturated in that pool. There was so much to see, feel and appreciate! It was an ideal time and place for me to meet Kanoe. I remember very little about that particular day other than the fascinating conversation that ensued.

I met Kanoe in a sort of roundabout way at the request of her human, whose name was Katherine. At first Katherine asked me to talk with her dog Benny, who was having some health challenges. In talking with Benny we learned that he attributed his poor health to the fact that he was carrying the energy of sadness for a human. It turned out that the sadness Benny spoke of was Katherine's and a big part of the sadness she felt was over her other dog, Kanoe. So I ultimately ended up talking with Kanoe to help Katherine come to a place of greater peace and understanding in regard to their life together.

Before I talked with Kanoe, I took a few moments to prepare myself as I do with any conversation. I try to do this with humans too. I simply take a few moments to just relax and focus on my breath so that I can easily move from what was on my mind previously to a momentary place of quiet. Let me explain here that our meeting was not in person in the physical sense — it was a telepathic meeting.

Once I felt I'd shifted my focus from my previous activity to a moment of quiet, I said hello to Kanoe. A smile just formed on my face as I write this now with the memory of how Kanoe instantly joined me on that day years ago and how I immediately began to feel her lively personality. You see, when we take a few moments to get quiet and greet an animal, plant, fellow human, the Earth or even a bug, we actually join as one in spirit. This can happen whether we are physically sitting close together or if we are speaking telepathically from opposite ends of the Earth. Although we can still feel our individual selves, we are joined together sharing in what our fellows of Nature term the "collective mind". We have access to all the experience and wisdom of the other and they have access to ours. When talking in this way, an animal will often look within me and comment on my personal experience or ask me to use something from my past to help humans understand their own experience.

When I greeted Kanoe, I felt the distinct presence of a dynamic individual with an incredible amount of energy and enthusiasm. I also noted that she was very happy and that she had a really unique slant on things. For instance, she had learned to open and get into the refrigerator and she found ways to get out in the neighborhood and roam around. Kanoe was very expressive of her sentiments toward individual humans and other animals. She was a wonderful friend and very engaging with most of them, but she could also be very aggressive with some individuals. There was no question about where she stood — she let you know right away. She was either your dearest loving companion the instant she met you and an entertaining clown, or she could appear to be a vicious attacker. She was a dog who, for many people, could be difficult to understand or to live with. She would create unusual challenges for Katherine that really pushed her to expand her awareness of herself and to grow personally.

Life with Kanoe was both a profound joy due to the depth of connection available with this amazing dog, and it was also stressful at times with what seemed like her unpredictable nature. In reality she was predictable, it was just that she might meet someone she wanted to share some wisdom with, which meant a bit of a wake-up call in the form of wisdom by aggression. She reminded me of a person who really spoke their mind. On one hand, this individual could be the most loving, kind person who expressed their appreciation for others' unique gifts and inspired and encouraged many. And then at times when they felt it was necessary, they might give a harsh attention-getting reminder to make a point to someone who was heading off their personal path. Kanoe was like that — her wisdom was shared based on her desire to help people find their way.

This sort of behavior and way of being may be accepted and even appreciated when it comes from a human, but unfortunately it is not acceptable when it comes from a dog. From the human standpoint with regard to the dog/human relationship, we feel the need to be in a position of control. This is where we might find our greatest challenges with our animal companions as they too, have their free will, and some of them tend to be free-spirited and challenge the human desire for control. When a dog shows aggression it is unacceptable to us and it makes sense. We humans don't usually take the time to really understand where a dog is coming from with their message of aggression, and most people don't even realize that a dog may have a message to share in the first place. But even if we really understand them, the fact may remain that this is the way the dog is and it may be impossible to maintain everyone's safety. The bottom line is that we don't know if a dog like Kanoe might seriously harm a child and we cannot take that chance. Sometimes simple measures can be put into place to allow a dog such as Kanoe to safely live in our human environment but sometimes, depending on the circumstances, even this can be impossible.

Some of the most amazing characters and friends we encounter along our journey of life, whether two-legged or four-legged, can be the ones who are the most challenging because they attempt to show us a different way of looking at our lives and a different way of living. We are often so caught up in our own way that it can be difficult to change course and live in a manner that might truly align with our own unique self as well as with that of our dog. With so much pressure to adhere to a certain lifestyle and rhythm as dictated by society, it can appear easier to simply conform. For Katherine, the magnitude of joy and love she felt living with an animal such as Kanoe made any inconvenient safety measures well worth it. Perhaps one day we will have the opportunity to get to know these individuals on a deeper level and be able to appreciate the love and wisdom they attempt to share at the expense of losing their freedom. I just want to take a moment here to express my gratitude for their presence as well as for those people with the patience and understanding to help these dogs find that sweet spot where they can live in safety in the environment we humans have created.

Katherine was one of those remarkable people and Kanoe had an enormous number of fans because of Katherine's gentle and careful way of sharing her dog with the community.

On this initial day of conversation with Kanoe I asked her for information and guidance to help Katherine overcome her profound sense of sadness and guilt because, despite Katherine's safety measures, Kanoe had managed to bite someone and was put to sleep. Katherine felt like she had killed her best friend and although it had been a year since Kanoe's death, she still felt the same level of intense pain and grief.

We began our session with Katherine asking all sorts of questions of Kanoe: What was your life like before I adopted you? Were you happy living with me? Why did you become aggressive? Do you know that I love you? Do you understand why I had you put to sleep? Will you forgive me?

Kanoe explained that she had experienced some rough

handling, what her previous humans thought of as rough play, in her early life. She said she felt very grateful for the experience of being part of Katherine's family and that she had never been so loved before. Kanoe said that her aggressive behavior was initiated in those early years and had been reinforced for what had been most of her life until Katherine adopted her when she was about five. She had learned to act aggressively and even to express love in an aggressive manner. When Kanoe was adopted into her new, loving home, she naturally became more expressive and more dynamic as she blossomed in this environment. Unfortunately this created many challenges, which ultimately resulted in her death.

Kanoe asked me to make it clear to Katherine that she understood the heart-wrenching decision Katherine was forced to make and how it pained her to this day. Kanoe demanded that I ask Katherine to promise that she would forgive herself. She thanked Katherine for the amazingly loving experience of being with her family and for making the difficult choice to send her home. Kanoe explained that she was happy to go home and to have the chance to begin again as a new puppy. She indicated that she was already back and living with a family with small children and that because of the wonderful learning experience she'd had with Katherine, she could now feel secure as a loving dog in a loving home. Kanoe wanted Katherine to know without a doubt how grateful she was for showing her that she could indeed live comfortably and joyfully with other people and animals. She went on to say that the experience of living with and leaving Katherine's family was a healing experience and that Katherine's promise to forgive herself would begin the process of healing for her, too.

Months later Katherine contacted me asking to talk with

Kanoe again. Let me share her email with you so that you can
understand where she was coming from and why she wanted to
reconnect with Kanoe.

Hi Maia,

Please tell Kanoe: "Every time I see a beautiful sunrise or
sunset I imagine you are part of it. You are in everything that
is beautiful and you will live on forever in my heart. I will
always love you and cherish our memories. Thank you!"

Maia, I was wondering what you think of a session
involving me asking Kanoe to give me her insight on anything
she wants or feels is necessary for me to know.

I have always believed that good comes out of all bad
situations. Sometimes you need to look for it a little harder
than other times, but it's always there. I seem to be realizing
more and more each day that I'm just not in the right place in
life. I have so much to offer this world and I have great
insight into many situations. There just doesn't seem to be a
place for me to share. I'm being lectured every second of the
work day by my customers. I do my best to keep my com-
posure and deal with them in an appropriate manner. I have
to tell you Maia, it gets very difficult not to give these guys
a dose of their own medicine or even worse — hang up on
them! It takes all my strength to keep what they say and how
they act from affecting my work.

Sometimes I wish I could pack up my dogs, buy a house
in the mountains or on the ocean, miles away from other
people so I could let them run and play SAFELY in the fresh
air, and spend my time rounding up all the men and women

who chose to engage their animals in the blood sport of pit fighting and any other form of animal abuse and lock them up forever!

Anyway, I would be curious to just sit back and listen to what Kanoe has to say about my life, her life, and the world as a whole!

You and Kanoe have been among my greatest teachers in life. I feel I could gain a lot by allowing her to speak on the subjects she feels are necessary, instead of being obligated to answer my questions. I wish I could do something in her honor — maybe she will offer some suggestions. Let me know what you think.

Thanks again, Maia!
Katherine

I responded:

Dear Katherine,

Kanoe is aware of your message to me. What follows is her response to your email. Let me know if you have any questions on this.

Thank you & love to you & your family!
Maia

As soon as Kanoe began to speak I sensed there was something unusual going on. I will never forget Kanoe's response to the topics mentioned in Katherine's email — to the questions that many of us have about life. I had no idea what I was about to hear and what I did hear profoundly changed my life and caused me to begin believing that these animals had valuable information to share, important not only for their particular humans, but for humanity as a whole.

Kanoe's message opened my eyes and because of it, I began gathering and saving conversations to one day share with my fellow humans. In sharing this message with you at last, I feel like I'm back in time when I met Kanoe and where I began to understand for the first time the magnitude of what I was privileged to be hearing. When I gave Kanoe the floor to speak, she really took it! She immediately surprised me with her opening statement; I had never heard an animal say anything like that before. I was still feeling the newness of this understanding when she made her second mind expanding announcement. Needless to say, I was all ears! Kanoe had certainly captured my attention!

I encourage you to read Katherine's email (above) once more before diving into Kanoe's dissertation as I believe it will add clarity to her words. What follows is an amazing conversation I had many years ago with a dog named Kanoe that strongly impacted me personally as well as my career as an Animal Communication Specialist.

A change has occurred and I am no longer a dog speaking to a human. I am here now as a dog representing the Grand Kingdom of Animal Creatures, the Great Family of Plants, the Wise and Interesting Association of Insects and the Grand Matter, fondly called Mother Earth. I have been asked to share a message not only with my woman but with all humans who have the desire to listen. The message is stimulated by the questions of my woman which also appear to be questions in the minds and hearts of many humans. At times I will appear to be speaking directly to my woman, but please keep in mind that I am speaking to all humans. Thank you!

First dear Woman, I would like to remind you that each human and each creature upon this planet is involved in their own evolution, their own remembering of who they are and their Divine connection. This exploration, as it were, comes in many forms and in many expressions. Some may represent what you term to be cruelty to animals, or an irritable customer. There are an infinite number of expressions and these are in the moment, ever changing.

The temptation of humans is to respond in a like manner, matching rudeness with rudeness, cruelty with cruelty. This is the easiest response, requiring only that we locate what we have in our own past, bringing it into the present and expressing it.

Our irritation in the first place is a sign that we have learned something about a particular issue and that we are now intolerant of it in ourselves or in others.

Many humans remain at this point and become champions, fighting against the injustice that was once each of yours, but that has been overcome. This can serve the purpose of bringing others over the hump, and it can serve to assist others in remaining even more firmly entrenched in their positions. In the larger picture of things, however, this approach does not serve to share and nurture light upon the planet; it merely perpetuates the darkness due to the fact that the basis for struggling on this level comes from fear rather than from love.

A good example lies in many what you term to be environmental or animal rights organizations. Their intent to protect and honor Nature and the marvelous creatures is honorable and Divine. But quite often the work of these organizations and individuals originates from fear of the loss of the creatures or the loss of the Earth, rather than from love.

It makes sense to come from fear, as the situation appears to be fearful; however, this merely perpetuates the challenges. If someone tries to stop another from exploiting Nature when coming from a state of fear, the person they are trying to stop will even more fearfully hold onto their desire to exploit. They are stimulated to feel fear at their base, which is often at the survival level for their families. They clutch even tighter onto what they think of as their right to exploit, without any reason. Or they hold on merely for the fact that someone or some organization is rudely trying to stop them.

On the other hand, when an individual or organization comes from a state of love, there is also the wisdom that comes along with it. I would like to talk about this wisdom, dear Woman, as it exists within you, as does the love.

This love is a glorious thing and it is what changes the world in a gentle, yet powerful way. This is what brings about lasting changes. In your daily interactions you have the grand opportunity to touch many fellow humans and animals alike.

Challenge yourself to not take what your fellow humans say personally, and remember that each human is dealing with his or her own journey. Decide what your journey is and decide to stay with it. What is being suggested is that you stay in the love and that you treat all other life forms with love, respect and kindness, no matter how rude or unappreciative they may be. We are not asking that you be a "doormat" as it were; on the contrary, we are suggesting that you speak your mind and your heart. But, you will feel your mind and thoughts changing if you make a pact each day to come from a place of love. By doing this any fear will be noted and worked through, and any frustration will be worked through by you without passing it on to another.

Become a transformer of negativity. When it comes in, take it and send the energy out as love. Experiment with this, Woman — it may add a new and interesting dimension to your workplace. Challenge yourself to be the end of the line in regard to negativity. Do not nurture negativity within yourself or others. When you think of others you would like to punish for doing what you term to be bad, challenge yourself to look at these people in a new way and realize that love, not hate, will change them for the better. It is not that you are being asked to accept what they are doing. You are being asked to tune in to your knowingness, to find a place of peace within you. Because when you tune in to your knowingness, you will see and you will feel that all is well.

When we come from hate and fear we often unknowingly encourage others to continue doing what they are doing and to hold onto it with a vengeance, if for no other reason than because others want them to stop what they are doing.

So, dear Woman, you are being asked to come from love and to move forward in your knowingness, rather than getting stuck in the judgment of others. When you observe fellow humans, remember that they are Divine and that each one of you, no matter how rude, has that divinity within. Challenge yourself to *see it and respond to it rather than to the negativity and anger.*

*With this awakening of awareness within you, Woman,
you may practice in your workplace until it becomes easy. Then
perhaps it will be time to follow a new passion. With this new
perspective, you will have more clarity on what it is that you so
wish to do. You will feel it strongly and will then merely need to
summon the courage to go after your dreams.*

*Take a little time to set into place a new way of viewing the
world. It will lighten your gloomy view. Realize, dear Woman,
that you humans create your tomorrows and yes, it is important
to notice and take steps to change what appears to be destructive to your glorious planet, but when you humans maintain a
vision of the destruction and injustices, you help to bring these
solidly into reality.*

*Dear Woman and dear Humans, hold the vision of Nature in
its pristine beauty in your minds to lovingly maintain its presence in your futures. Hold the vision of love, of equality and of
peace. See it and make note of it each day. It is all around you
in your lives. Celebrate the love, equality and peace! Make it
grand! Feel it within your very being for this is how you make
it a reality. There are so many wonderful examples, but all you
often see is the negative, the destruction and the violence.*

*See the beauty of the interactions you have with each
other — walks with friends, the peace of washing the dishes,
the satisfaction of having a cozy home. Appreciate the magic
and the wisdom that surrounds and envelops you each precious
moment of each glorious day. Allow this to be the reality for you
every day, for it exists all around and in you. And let it be your,
what you term to be future, because what you feel and know*

today will be your tomorrows. Pass it on by being the love and by being the wisdom, by being the peace and the grace in all your interactions.

Dear humans, when you come from love, you don't come from fear. Love is what changes the world in the ways that I think you want to see the world change.

After taking a few moments to pause and reflect on Kanoe's incredible message, I sent it off in an email to Katherine. About a week later I received a response back:

Hi Maia,

Thank you Maia, for communicating with my animals. I am going through a bad time right now; our business is in jeopardy of closing its doors and I'm feeling very stressed. But somehow whenever I hear from my dogs and try to expand on their wisdom, as well as yours, I start to feel better. I just wish I could keep this feeling all the time!! Thank you from the bottom of my heart. Without you to teach me and others about the true meaning of life, I may have never really known how amazing it could be to simply take a walk with my dogs!!! That's what life is about, those peaceful times, not all the negativity that clutters our lives and thinking patterns. Thank You!!

Sorry I haven't responded sooner to Kanoe's message. I loved it! I thought everything she had to say made perfect sense. The only thing I struggle with is where to draw the line with patience and love. I will never be a doormat, but it's difficult to know how and when to solve conflict while staying

210

"in the love" that Kanoe describes. I have tested her theory at work and I have been pleasantly surprised at the responses I have gotten.

Maia, I would be truly honored if you would share these words with the world. Kanoe is a grand soul and through your sacred voice of communication, she always will be my guide to peace, love and happiness. Both you and Kanoe have changed my life forever. You have given me direction and purpose. I never had these things before. I notice the difference in the environment I'm in by changing my perception of it. It is almost like magic. You can change an angry, stressful situation to a room full of laughter and lightheartedness in a split second. It is a choice. I don't choose to be angry anymore, I choose to love instead.

I'm a better person because of it and so are the people around me. It isn't easy and in fact I slipped today in the office. But I'm aware now and because of the awareness, I can change a mood that even I created — in a heartbeat!

Kanoe will always live on in my heart and I will continue to miss her. I will honor Kanoe as my guide and teacher and hope she can change the life of others. Nothing would make me happier than to know she made a difference to someone else. I know Kanoe has a grand desire, and I trust that her wishes will be fulfilled through your help.

Thank you for everything Maia and I return the love and light to you and yours. You are truly blessed!

Thanks again, Maia!
Katherine

After I received Katherine's email, I decided to go right to Kanoe for more answers. I took a few deep, slow, relaxing breaths and then called out to her. Kanoe, are you available to talk? Are you aware of the questions of your woman?

Yes, thank you, Woman!

I would like to respond to the question about where to draw the line with patience and love.

If you check in with yourself regularly to ask where you are coming from — love or fear — you will begin to feel a grand difference. If you are angry, you are coming from fear rather than love. When you set your intent on coming from love rather than from fear, you will feel a sense of peace, and a sense of knowing that comes from choosing love. And more than anything you will feel a new patience and understanding that no matter how bad things may seem or look, all is and will be well.

Love creates the wisdom to value the sacredness of the planet, the sacredness of all life and of each precious interaction. When we think, act and speak from a basis of love, we value each breath, each moment. When we have this appreciation, we see and feel the magic of life and we treat all with equal respect and kindness. We live as representatives of the light, of the love.

Do you see that without the love there is no awareness of the wisdom — that there is no awareness of the natural understanding which is unquestionably true and that exists within each being of life? Without the love, there is no connection with that wisdom that each human and each creature of life has deep within. Fear blocks the awareness of this wisdom.

Humans are parleying on the most superficial levels —

dancing about with all kinds of fear. There is fear of destroying the planet you call Earth and its glorious creatures, fear of being able to survive in some, and the use of fear in the desire to control in others.

There are those desiring to protect the Earth based on fear of her destruction. They are deeply touched by the beauty of the planet and by her creatures, but nonetheless they too come from a stance of fear, of anger and even of hatred for those who come from a different perspective.

There are those who supposedly exploit Nature based on the simple need and desire to support their families. These humans respond with fear for their own survival and with fear of losing their freedom when they feel the fear of organizations and individuals that want them to stop exploiting Nature.

And there are those humans who play the game of exploitation, of competition, merely for the game — to win riches and to be the victor. These humans play on the fears of the humans who want to protect the Earth and pit them against those wishing to focus on the immediate survival of themselves and their families.

The humans involved in the game live for the game. They are not living in fear for the Earth or its creatures or for their fellow humans. They truly are not in the battle, but are playing off the emotions and fears of the Earth lovers and the simple families wanting to support themselves. The game players represent those in control based on the naivety of the other factions. Does this make sense?

What I, what we of the animal kingdom — truly the kingdom of all life — wish to point out is the position of each of the *opposing human factions. Humans are so deeply focused on their beliefs and their fears and on the battles they create based on these beliefs and fears that they fail to see the larger vision.*

The humans with the most control are the ones who have the ability to look at the situation and come from a place of peace and a place of wisdom, rather than from fear. But these humans are few and far between.

Perhaps those with the most clarity are the ones playing the game. They have an emotional detachment that allows them to sit back and look at the situation with a wider vision as though they're looking at a game board. Meanwhile, the other organizations and small exploiters are like pawns on the board deeply enmeshed in their particular plights. The game players don't necessarily come from love or from peace, but neither do they come from desperation or fear. They are able to see the larger picture and manipulate those with a great appreciation for the Earth, who are deep in their fears about the future of the Earth and her magnificent creatures. The game players are also able to manipulate those who exploit on a smaller scale, often pitting the environmentally focused against the small-scale exploiters in an effort for control and as a diversion while they — the game players — are actually the large-scale exploiters.

The Kingdom of Life represented by the Animal Kingdom and here represented by one dog, would like to bring these facts to the awareness of those who bestow such love and appreciation upon our sweet beings, and we would like to recommend that the factions of Earth-loving humans bond with the factions of simple people desiring to protect their families and to survive. Bond in a love for life, for what is basic, and for what is good.

And, we would also recommend that these entities cease the battle. This is very important! Stop battling! This is the most challenging aspect for you humans to grasp.

It is not a matter of closing your mouths and your eyes to what is going on. It is about gaining a deeper understanding of the truth.

It is about asking the Earth in your quiet moments. It is about asking the creatures in the stillness and listening to the truth and feeling it deep within your being. What is the way? How do we best move forward and what action, if any, do we take?

What is being done is not working. What has been done has not worked. Perhaps there is a way that has not yet been considered, a way that is expansive and alive, a way that is based on the wisdom of the magic of the very life that is being appreciated and the one that humans want to preserve. Perhaps it is based on the wisdom of Nature itself.

Whenever action is taken based on fear, it is hurtful to all life. Understand, dear Humans, that actions or words based on fear only add to the fire of what you term to be destruction. And that whenever humans imagine the Earth or her creatures in destruction, they help to make this a reality. Your imaginings are so important!

If you humans would place your thoughts on images of the Earth as a healthy pristine environment teeming with life, this would be the most helpful, the most powerful thing you can do. And, seek to bond with fellow humans in your commonalities. The result will be even more powerful if a number of humans thought of and imagined the Earth in vibrant health and felt the profound gratitude and joy of these imaginings.

Do you not see, dear Humans, how you create your environments, your reality, and your very lives by the thoughts and by the images that you choose to hold in your minds and in your hearts? These thoughts and images are your visions and they create your tomorrows.

And now we of the Kingdom of Life upon this planet wish to express a truth that we find to be disturbing and perplexing.

The humans who love the Earth and who appreciate her grand beauty and that of her creatures are the very ones who have the opportunity to keep her vibrantly alive in all her splendor. They carry the visions of her beauty in their spirits and in their hearts, being intimately aware of her magic.

This wonderful group of humans feels the magic that she has to offer, but most of them fail to use this magic as wisdom in their desire to keep the magic alive. It is quite similar to those humans who feel a deep connection with the Earth's creatures, but fail to gather wisdom from us to use in our preservation.

These well-intentioned humans are filled with love and appreciation for what is termed to be Nature, but are also equally filled with fear for our possible destruction and they are full of hatred for fellow humans who might cause any harm to Nature.

In their ignorance, many humans who fight for our protection and survival unfortunately and unknowingly also create the greatest harm to the planet and to its creatures. This is true because these humans hold a vision of Nature within themselves, but rather than holding the vision of Nature in its pristine form, rather than noticing all the beauty and the positive aspects each day, they see the garbage and the destruction and hold these images in their minds and in their hearts.

This population of humans has the potential to be most powerful in the preservation of the planet, due to the deep connection that they have to it, but based on their choice to come from fear rather than love, they hold the vision of destruction of Nature rather than the vibrant liveliness of it.

This is why it appears to you Earth-loving humans that you are losing the battle. The more of you who learn environmental education from a negative standpoint and the more humans who gather to hold the vision of destruction, the more destruction will occur. That is and will continue to be your reality.

Imagine how many humans hold the image of destruction in their minds and in their hearts daily because they have chosen to come from fear. Imagine how powerful this is, how destructive this is, knowing that you are the humans who consciously think about the Earth and all her creatures more often each day than any other humans. You humans truly have the life of the Earth and her inhabitants in your hands! It is not about battling others. They don't need to be battled. In fact, they don't think about the Earth much. You are the ones who could so easily change the world if you would only change your minds!

We ask that you humans feel the power you have. Be careful and conscious of what you decide to hold in your thoughts and in your minds.

Yes, have your eyes open to what is happening; yes, speak out, but do it out of love and peace rather than fear. You may think there is no time for love or for peace. On the contrary, there is no time for fear; stop it immediately and choose to see and to know the magic and the magnificence of Nature each day, each moment in all its vitality. Live in the magic of its presence and know that it will always continue.

The planet is incredibly powerful. The force of all life and all creatures is magnificent. It will respond to your images of vitality, as it has to those images of destruction. You will see more and more examples of the vitality of life as you awaken your vision of it.

We of the grand Kingdom of Life do not support battles, even and especially in our name. We know the destructiveness of doing this. We see that those without a vision are currently in control and that those who dearly love the Earth and all the grand creatures are supporting the destruction of the planet and its creatures by living in the image of fear and destruction. Do you see this? This is so important!

You lovers of Earth! You appreciators of the grandness of her beauty and wisdom and of the magic of all the unique creatures of life! We beseech you to sit upon a rock, to sit within Nature and to look deep within your soul and ask yourselves if this is not true.

We ask that you align yourself to the truth that the Earth is powerful, that the Earth is vibrantly alive and incredibly beautiful in all her wisdom. We ask you to see and to feel the energy of love, which cradles and nurtures all life. We ask that you choose to hold this as your truth if you feel it strongly within you, that you notice each sign of the vibrant essence of life each moment of each day, and that you choose to live in this wisdom. We ask that you choose to be powerful in deciding that this is what you want, and that this is what you know in order to support the image of the vibrant essence of life upon Earth.

We also ask that you choose to bravely examine your fears, your anger and to work through them, refraining from imposing them on anyone, even and especially those who you think to be your enemies.

And, we ask that you decide that you have no enemies. Know that all are working toward different goals but that all can be satisfied with an understanding of a grander vision.

Take ownership for your part in creating the destruction of Nature, because each one of you humans has contributed in your own way.

Stop judging others. Do your part, knowing that the most powerful thing any of you can do now, in this moment and forever more — is to preserve the image of Nature and of the planet in all its magnificence. Spread the word to fellow lovers of the Earth to hold the image of life, of beauty and of love. Hold the space of the Earth in all its vitality, for in this way, you nourish her and make a conscious choice to keep her alive now and forever.

You will see it as your reality. See it each moment of each day. Choose to see it. Choose to create it! You have a choice!

We beseech you to use the power you have each moment in choosing your thoughts and choosing your images to preserve the planet in all its glory. So be it!

Find the sweetness of humanity every day,
even if it seems like a tiny thing.

Find it and feel it in your heart. It could be something
on the television or radio, some good deed. It could be
some kindness given to another in the market or on
the highway. It is there! It is everywhere to be seen
and felt because humans are basically good and
kind-hearted beings. It is confusion and lack of self
love that bring about unkind acts; the more that
humans focus on violence, the more unkind and
horrific acts will occur. Your human information-
sharing is aligned toward sharing violent events and
acts. But there are even more profound acts of kind-
ness each day, yet they often fail to be acknowledged.

The vibrant health of your species depends on remembering the profound love that exists within each human and giving this love the kind of attention it deserves. We suggest that you celebrate it all the time — each day — and to welcome this truth into your reality. It resides in the hearts of all. Why not allow it to be felt and known on a wider scale? If you imagine a dog such as myself and others of my kind, the most common image is of love. We exude it and we celebrate it because that is what we are!

We are love — and so are you!

– Calvin

DOGS SAY THE DARNDEST THINGS

You can talk with and listen to animals too!
For information on awakening your natural abilities to
listen to dogs and other wise beings of Nature contact:

Maia Kincaid Ph.D.
Wisdom of Love Publishing
www.maiakincaid.com
www.holisticintuition.com
P.O. Box 4761
Sedona, AZ 86340
928- 282-0768

All available through: www.maiakincaid.com

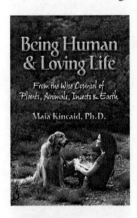
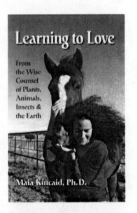
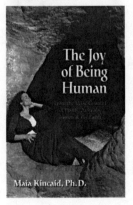

CPSIA information can be obtained at www.ICGtesting.com
Printed in the USA
LVOW11s1543231213

366580LV00002B/304/P